Nature, Culture, and History

Nature, Culture, and History

The "Knowing" of Oceania

K. R. Howe

University of Hawai'i Press
Honolulu

00 01 02 03 04 05   5 4 3 2 1

Library of Congress Cataloging-in-Publication Data

Howe, K. R.
Nature, culture, and history : the "knowing" of Oceania / K. R. Howe.
p. cm.
Rev. and extended versions of the three lectures presented at
Massey University, Palmerston North and Albany campuses, in 1997,
as the "Macmillan Brown lectures," organized by the Macmillan Brown
Centre for Pacific Studies at the University of Canterbury.
Includes bibliographical references and index.
Contents: Introduction — Nature as culture —
Culture as nature — History as culture.
ISBN 0–8248–2286–2 (cloth : alk. paper) —
ISBN 0–8248–2329–X (paper : alk. paper)
1. Oceania. I. Title: "Knowing" of Oceania. II. Title.
DU17.H69 2000
995—dc21   99–087297

Book design by Kenneth Miyamoto
Printed by The Maple-Vail Book Manufacturing Group

For Robin Fisher
(il miglior fabbro)
who led us into the cold

Contents

Preface

THIS STUDY has its origins in 1994 when, thanks to Robin Fisher and the University of Northern British Columbia, my family and I spent some time in central British Columbia, Canada. Having never been beyond a temperate or tropical zone before, I found living in temperatures typically of minus 30 degrees centigrade an exciting novelty. I was surprised to find that it was relatively easy to live "normally" in the cold, something that many northern cultures have of course been doing successfully for many thousands of years. I read about the development of modern Canadian cultural characteristics and the pervasive influence of a vast, cold landscape. It soon dawned on me that the Canadian "wilderness" and the "cold" were as much ideas as some sort of physical actuality. This led me to questions about, and a huge literature on, the influence of the environment on human personality and culture more generally, and, conversely, the way in which human societies represented the natural world. In the light of this, I thought again about Western responses to "my" temperate and tropical part of the world—Oceania.

This research was given a jolt by a postcard from Robert Hoskins and finally shape and purpose when I was invited by the Board of the Macmillan Brown Centre for Pacific Studies at the University of Canterbury to present the Macmillan Brown Lectures. I thank the board very much for this honor. The three chapters in this book are revised and extended versions of those three lectures, presented at Massey University's Palmerston North and Albany campuses in 1997.

At Massey University I am indebted to Robert Hoskins and David Thomson for their helpful comments. I also thank many friends and colleagues for the organization and support for the Macmillan Brown Lectures, and in particular Glynnis Cropp, Peter Lineham, and John Muirhead. I also thank Massey University for a Research Fellowship and the Australian National University for a Visiting Fellowship, both in 1998, which enabled preparation of the lectures for publication. At the ANU I received very kind support from Donald Denoon, Brij Lal, and Hank Nelson. Anonymous readers' reports from University of Hawai'i Press are also greatly appreciated. I am grateful to Nigel Brown for permission to use his wonderful painting, which is so redolent of many of the themes of this book, on the cover.

Above all, I am grateful to Robin Fisher, Mary-Ellen Kelm, and the University of Northern British Columbia for an experience of a lifetime.

Introduction

HOW DO WE KNOW what we see? Why do we know what we know? These questions are as old as the human species. In the postmodern/postcolonial world in which historians and other scholars now claim to operate, a critical (though not original) assumption is that the external world, both past and present, is necessarily viewed and interpreted through cultural lenses. This is not to suggest, as some extremists do, that the external world does not exist, just that the *interpretation* of "reality" is likely to be a product of the observer's cultural positioning, whose depiction of it will be in culturally specific language. There is no neutral or value-free observation post. In this sense knowledge is created by different cultural groups for different purposes rather than being empirically discovered, fixed and true for all times and all observers.

This book considers processes of "seeing" and "knowing" by discussing concepts of nature, culture, and history with reference to Oceania. The words *nature* and *culture* are among the most problematic in our language, and I have no wish to define them at length. For my simplistic working purposes here, I take nature to be the varied and changing constructions of the environment humans inhabit, or are aware of, and the forces that are deemed to operate upon it. Culture I define as the constitution, practices, and beliefs of human societies. By history I mean representations of the past.

Oceania, or the world of the Pacific islands, is as much a

rhetorical device, an intellectual artifact, as it is a physical or cultural location. Knowledge about the natural world of the Pacific islands and their cultures and histories largely derives from a complex range of Western ideas and assumptions. Much Western understanding of Oceania is culturally constructed, mediated, and organized. But rather than simply state this fairly obvious deconstructionist generalization, I wish to emphasize the importance of specific location and contingency for Oceania. I am particularly interested in the interplay between Western theories about nature and culture (such as religious, geographic, environmental, ethnographic, anthropological, and biological) and the raw materials of experience, observation, and expectation, past, present, and future.

Over the past two hundred or more years, Oceania has been a major Western ideological testing ground. Ideas and questions about human "civilization," the relationships between nature and culture, racial classification and culture contact, cultural and biological survival and destiny have all been extensively tested and examined using Pacific case studies. Thus the islands of the Pacific Ocean have not only been economically and politically colonized by the West, but, perhaps more profoundly, they have been intellectually occupied and conceptually shaped by the West. And, in turn, experiences in and observations of the Pacific have sometimes influenced Western understandings of itself.

Chapter 1, "Nature as Culture," examines the origins and evolution of a particular Western cultural site—namely, a tropical Pacific island, or rather the *idea* of such an island. I consider how island worlds have been variously reconstituted to reflect Western cultural expectations. I argue that the common modern depiction of the Pacific islands as paradise has its distant origins in Indo-European and Arabic philosophies and that early Western images of paradise eventually coalesced around the idea of the tropical island. These images, I suggest, were imported into the Pacific by the earliest Spanish explorers and were in existence in the Pacific some hundreds of years before the Cook voyages, with which we most tend to associate such images. I then trace how from the later eighteenth century into the early twentieth century, the Pacific islands were depicted as the very opposite of paradise and became instead in Western minds places of fear and loathing. The modern re-representation of the ideal tropical Pacific island paradise, I argue, is a product of twentieth-century thinking, which has to do with the changing relationship between nature and culture as explanatory paradigms. I suggest that the discourse of twentieth-century tourism, with its colonialist underpinnings, is one way of seeing this recreation of today's images of the Pacific as paradise.

Chapter 2, "Culture as Nature," is to some extent the obverse of this argument. I consider how culture has been variously interpreted in relationship to nature. My purpose is to examine a fundamental shift in Western thinking about the nature of human culture over the last two hundred years. That shift involves the development and then rejection of the notion, prevalent by and especially during the nineteenth century, that somehow the natural world determined culture and an acceptance of the more recent concept that culture is more independent of its natural environment and more able to determine itself. The study of Oceanic societies, I argue, not only illustrates this changing paradigm, but it also helped to provide critical evidence for the shifting positions. The chapter ends by posing some questions about whether today's culture-centric world of history, anthropology, sociology, and their mutated offspring such as cultural, gender, and consciousness studies have become trapped in a closed loop of explanation. Has culture been reduced merely to a text, and considered outside nature altogether?

Chapter 3, "History as Culture," turns the spotlight onto the history of the Pacific. It examines how Westerners have constructed such history and considers the extent to which it, like the concepts of nature and culture, similarly reflects Western expectations. I suggest that all Pacific history, old and new, is an ongoing morality tale, fundamentally about the idea of Western civilization, its perceived rise and fall, its fears and triumphs, and its creation of a Pacific Other onto which are projected and tested the West's various priorities and expectations. I question whether there really is an essential difference between imperial and so-called postcolonial Pacific history. I suggest that the self-proclaimed radicalism of "new" theoretical approaches needs to be read against a two-century-long history of Western engage-ment with Oceania. While the specific concerns and interpreta-tions of Pacific historians may have changed dramatically over two hundred years, from such issues as civilization, imperial destiny, and race survival to matters such as racism, sexism, environmentalism, and political rights, the fundamental pro-cesses and purposes of such representation remain surprisingly similar. We may now "know" Oceania differently, but it must not be assumed, as it commonly is, that we know it better.

Some final introductory comments. While my Macmillan Brown Lectures have been extended and revised for this book, I have tried to retain something of their original rhetorical flavor. Also, I have been interested though not surprised that of the very many individuals who helpfully commented on the lectures and on these chapters in draft form, most have addressed issues in chapter 3. While acknowledging the significance of "reader response theory," I would like to say that I think the main con-tribution of this book is summarized in the final section of chap-ter 2 and that the discussion of history in chapter 3 is exem-plary. In other words, chapter 3 should not be read in isolation.

Chapter 1

Nature as Culture

It seemed like the worst of times. I had too much teaching, too many committees, and it was mid-winter in New Zealand's Palmerston North—miserable, wet, with incessant gales. Hail was shattering onto my office windows at the exact moment that I received a postcard from my colleague Robert Hoskins, who was holidaying in Tonga. The card was a picture of Fafa Island resort. Within a few weeks, and at great expense, I was with my family for a week's holiday on Fafa. There is nothing remarkable about this story, you might think, other than my impulsive and uncharacteristic splashing out of lots of money. The whole point of Pacific island tourism is to attract people to sunny, warm islands of paradise.

What are these Pacific tourist images so vividly expressed in brochures? What do they convey? Typically they offer *difference* from our everyday lives—promising leisure, indolence, abandonment, a strong hint of sexuality, in a warm climate with endless blue skies, azure seas, shimmering white sand, foaming coral reefs, stunningly colored lagoons, waving palm trees. There is no wind and rain. There are no crowds. There is no work. There are no responsibilities. There is absolutely nothing to worry about. Everything is warm and safe. Everything is provided. Fafa is every tropical Pacific island.

These images and experiences are at once both very simple and also very complex. An island like Fafa is a modern Western cultural site, but it also has very ancient Western cultural ori-

5

gins. It is a world my cultural memory makes me expect to find and thus pleasurably and successfully anticipate. Both nature and culture are prepackaged, sanitized, controlled, and safe. It is a colonialist enterprise in its assumptions. The visitor's experience of the indigenous culture, if it exists at all, tends to be little more threatening than sleeping in a thatched hut and perhaps attending a floor show. Islanders are happy and eager to serve with a smile. The island experience will be brief, and a return to the normal world is guaranteed. Friends are then bored with your photos as you relive the experience.

How has this come about? And, knowing it, why would a cynical Pacific islands historian behave the way I did in response to a fifty-cent postcard? I am not, I would have thought, a typical island tourist. I've spent thirty years studying and writing about the Pacific and have spent considerable time living and traveling around the islands. Much of my writing has investigated and challenged the Romantic myths and ideals about the islands. I *know* that the Pacific islands are not in fact an earthly paradise and that collectively they have complex histories and cultures and, in particular, have all kinds of major socioeconomic, cultural, political, and environmental problems associated with their smallness, lack of resources, isolation, urbanization, and especially their experiences of colonization and decolonization. I also know that the sun does not always shine. Yet in spite of all my "rational" learning, knowing that the Romantic images were not "real," knowing that I was compromised in a colonialist enterprise and mentality, there I was still prepared to pay good money to chase after them. I willingly played a cultural role, as cosseted tourist, as primeval man going back to a peaceful, safe, restorative nature.

Until fairly recently, I uncritically accepted the common view that modern Western images of the Pacific islands spring directly from the literature of later-eighteenth-century voyages, particularly those of Cook with Banks and of Bougainville, which depicted Tahiti in particular as an earthly paradise of ease, tropical abundance, and unbridled eroticism. "One would think himself in the Elysian fields," wrote Bougainville. "I thought I was transported into the garden of Eden; we crossed a turf covered with fine fruit trees, and intersected by little rivulets, which kept up a pleasant coolness in the air."[1] Bougainville's Tahiti was La Nouvelle Cythère—the home of Venus: "the very air the people breathe, their songs, their dances, all conspire to call to mind the sweets of love, and all engage to give themselves up to them."[2] From the Cook voyages comes this oft-quoted account by Banks:

> [We] walked for 4 or 5 miles under groves of Cocoa nut and bread fruit trees loaded with a profusion of fruit and giving the most grateful shade I have ever experienced, under these were the habitations of the people most of them without walls: in short the scene we saw was the truest picture of an arcadia of which we were going to be kings that the imagination can form. . . . these happy people may almost be said to be exempt from the curse of our forefather; scarcely can it be said that they earn their bread with the sweat of their brow when their cheifest sustenance Bread fruit is procured with no more trouble than that of climbing a tree and pulling it down.[3]

Even in New Zealand, colder and "wilder" than tropical Pacific islands, Arcadia might exist. Parkinson thought that Tolaga Bay with its woods and fresh waters was "agreeable beyond description . . . [and] with proper cultivation, might be rendered a kind of second Paradise."[4]

These images and their astonishing effect on the European reading public have received more than a generation of intense study, most notably by Bernard Smith in his *European Vision and the South Pacific* and his numerous other works.[5] Here I am more interested in both the antecedents of these later-eighteenth-century images and those that have followed. My starting assumption, recently (though by no means originally) expressed by Simon Shama in his *Landscape and Memory*, is that "landscapes are culture before they are nature."[6]

The idea of paradise

The most common word applied to Pacific islands by outsiders is "paradise." An explanation goes back a long way into Western cultural memory.

Many early Indo-European societies invented mythical golden ages of bounteous nature, perpetual springtime, and peace between humans and beasts. Judeo-Christian tradition had men and women created in paradise, specifically the Garden of Eden, later to be driven out into a world of sin, pain, work, and danger. The idea of an earthly paradise lasted for a long time in Christian doctrines. Christian notions blended readily with more carnal Greek concepts of Arcadia, where one might find dancing, wine drinking, and lovemaking to sweet music in pastoral settings, and Elysium, an underground afterlife. As with so much of Greek mythology, concepts of paradise were derived from early Indian (Sanskrit) mythology. Earliest Western locations of paradise were either in India or somewhere "in the East."[7] The question of location was contentious. Was paradise allegorical or real? Had it survived the Flood? Did it still exist? Did it contain the wealth of King Solomon? Could it be recreated? The tree-planting schemes and botanic gardens of late medieval times in Egypt, India, and Arab countries were conscious efforts to recreate an earthly paradise in a context of spiritual philosophy and medicinal and botanic science. They were the forerunners of the great botanic gardens of sixteenth- and seventeenth-century Europe, by which time the idea of actually finding the original earthly paradise not too far away had faded.[8]

But such hopes were rekindled for many when Spain and Portugal eventually traveled eastward to India and beyond and westward to the Americas. The Dutch, French, and British soon followed. European expansion on this unprecedented global scale was a product of new maritime technology and navigational knowledge, combined with the psychological and economic imperatives of developing nation-states in search of new domains, particularly the riches of India and China. At heart, however, lay the "'search for Eden'—a phenomenon whose roots lay in a complex of European, Arabic and Indian philosophical traditions."⁹ The Renaissance emphasis on the golden age of Greek classical tradition sharpened the imaginative landscape of paradise. The Reformation spiced its politico-religious dimensions, while the rise of capitalism intensified the prospect of riches. New learning fed on new discoveries in nature. Eden/ Arcadia was now more specifically an earthly botanical paradise, a place offering the prospect of Christian domination, and, it was hoped, it would be littered with gold.

As the explorers pushed around the coasts of Africa to India and began to open the American continents, they constantly found, though not quite, such a paradise/Eden/Eldorado. Columbus, motivated more than most by such a search,[10] first thought he had found it in the West Indies. There he believed that the earth, which he thought pear-shaped rather than spherical, had a protuberance "like a woman's nipple."[11] Paradise was at the nipple's summit, from whence ran the great rivers to the rest of the world. Virtually every Spanish and Portuguese commander in Central and South America almost found it, as did the English in their early American colonies. Typical were the descriptions in 1502 by Amerigo Vespucci, who explored the Atlantic coastline of South America for Portugal:

> This land is very pleasant, and full of countless very large green trees which never shed their leaves, all giving off the sweetest aromatic fragrances, and produce infinite kinds of fruits excellent to the taste and healthy to the body. And the fields produce many sweet and delicious herbs, flowers, and roots, and sometimes . . . I thought I must be near the Earthly Paradise. . . . [The people] have no law or religious faith, they live as nature dictates, they do not know of the immortality of the soul. They have no private property among them, for they share everything. They have no borders of kingdoms or provinces; neither have they a king or anyone to obey: each is his own master. They do not administer justice, which is not necessary for them, since greed does not prevail among them.[12]

This was almost three hundred years before Banks, Bougainville, and others said identical things about Tahiti.

The idea of the tropical oceanic island

Notions of paradise in this age of European expansion also became linked to another popular concept—the tropical oceanic island—which was established in the European imagination hundreds of years before European sailors effectively explored the Pacific ocean.[13]

The linking of paradise with such islands had many imaginative precedents. Settings for political utopias were often islands—probably because they were small and offered the ready possibility of visibility and control, as opposed to the difficulties of containment and protection in continental locations. Islands are also surrounded by sea, which could have physical and moral cleansing and redemptive characteristics, and of course a journey was always required to get to an island thus connotating the elements of pilgrimage and adventure. Greek and early medieval utopias were often on islands.[14] Dante's *Purgatorio* has a redemptive paradise, accessed through the Devil's anus at the center of the earth, set on an island in the southern hemisphere, directly opposite Jerusalem.[15] More's *Utopia* of 1516 was set vaguely in the Pacific region. But the link between islands and paradises arose naturally enough since islands are what the seekers of paradises first found: the West Indies, the islands off the west of Africa (Canaries, Madeira, St. Helena), and in the Indian Ocean (Mauritius). Columbus found Caribbean islands

> very lovely and green and fertile. . . . All is as green and the vegetation is as that of Andalusia in April. . . . The singing of little birds is such that it seems that a man could never wish to leave this place; the flocks of parrots darken the sun, and there are large and small birds of so many different kinds and so unlike ours, that it is a marvel. There are, moreover, trees of a thousand types, all with their various fruits and all scented, so that it is a wonder.[16]

He described the inhabitants as "naked," "timid," "guile-less," "generous," and "content," with a potential to become affectionate servants of Spain, Christians, and to "collect and give us the things they have in abundance which are necessary to us."[17] One could quote similar descriptions of islands such as Mauritius and St. Helena.[18]

Islands played many roles. They were places of safety, refuge, recreation, and reprovisioning for mariners. They had strategic, economic, colonial possibilities. They offered the exotic—new vegetation, new animals, new human cultures. They engendered notions of the fantastic and the inversion of values. Did men in such distant places have tails, dogs' heads? Were their feet around the other way (the origin of antipodes)? Were there giants? Such fabulations profoundly influenced travelers' expectations and the published accounts of their journeys. Columbus had read and was inspired by Greek and biblical geographic knowledge, medieval maps, and the highly embellished travel accounts of the likes of Marco Polo (who sent Columbus specifically looking for the Great Khan in China) and the outrageous John Mandeville (who claimed to have traveled around the world in the fourteenth century).[19] This early travel literature was important: successive generations of travelers relied upon it and so went with a sense of the expected. What characterized this "knowing" was not just what to us is the rather absurd nature of the "information," but a pre-Enlightenment "cognitive apparatus" and a classificatory system that was convincingly "derived from utterly fabulous authorities."[20]

Conversely, travelers' tales inspired more consciously literary works.[21] Not only were islands the locations of castaways and cannibals, buccaneers and pirates and the inspiration of a literary tradition, which still exists, of adventure, privation, and wealth beyond imagining, but islands became allegorical sites and rhetorical devices. Perhaps the two most notable examples are Shakespeare's *Tempest* (1623), and Defoe's *Robinson Crusoe* (1719). *The Tempest* was inspired in part by Montaigne's essay on "cannibals" and by numerous published voyages, including one of a castaway in the Bermudas. It dealt with a range of heady issues: the natural and the supernatural, nature and art, the savage and the civilized, the colonizer and the colonized, and engaged in debate about ideal sociopolitical organization. The archetype island story, *Robinson Crusoe*, was based in part on the experiences of castaway Alexander Selkirk on Juan Fernandez in 1709. Defoe, who resites the island in the Caribbean, turns the story into one of Western capitalism's more influential manuals for individual self-effort and economic progress and domination. It is also about personal salvation, imperial energy, and racial master-servant relationships. More broadly in this context, it is argued that the extensive "discursive formations" around islands, especially in terms of colonialism and imperialism are not *a* theme in British/European literary history, but are "literary representations of *the* theme of British colonialism."[22]

But islands are more than literary devices and vehicles for political debate, satire, and imperial public relations. For the Western mind, it seems, they are also psychological spaces, offering the promise of safety and a control over destiny, as well as the promise of travel and adventure. Children, for example, are thus often attracted to the idea of islands, a form of circumscribed/enclosed place, like a hidey-hole or tree hut—to quote Ernst Bloch, the child's "wishful land is an island."[23] If one dared delve further into the psyche, perhaps the island offers a subconscious womblike experience. As adults, the fascination for being abandoned on a desert island relates, I think, to fundamental human questions: who am I in essence, what am I without the trappings of my society?[24]

Island paradises in Oceania

Peoples of Europe had long speculated about what lay on the other side of the world. There were early Greek and Christian speculations of a southern land mass. One bitter theological debate was whether humans could cross the so-called torrid zones to reach it or would melt in the attempt. By the twelfth century it was generally accepted that there was probably a huge southern land to balance the European/North African/ Asian landmass. Theoretical geographers claimed that it would be a fabulously wealthy place and named it Terra Australis Incognita. During the sixteenth century, with the tentative outlining of the Asian and American continents, Terra Australis was deemed to lie between them.[25] The Spanish made forays out from their new empires in the Americas, seeking its wealth and intent on saving the souls of its benighted inhabitants.[26]

Those travelers who began to enter the Oceanic world in the sixteenth century did so with a well-established mental landscape of the tropical island paradise—sweet airs, glorious abundance of flora and fauna, running fresh water, riches, and their human inhabitants living in a natural innocence and ready for co-option in imperial designs. Alvaro de Mendaña thought he had found Terra Australis in 1568. The islands still bear the Biblical name Solomons. On his second voyage he attempted to found a godly, utopian colony on the nearby Santa Cruz Islands. Quiros came upon the New Hebrides in 1605 where he attempted to found a great city—the New Jerusalem. Accounts of these and other early Pacific voyages spawned scores of utopian conjectures with Pacific island locations from the seventeenth century,[27] leading eventually to the most famous of all—*Gulliver's Travels.* What is remarkable about these early Spanish visits is that in spite of the hostility and many instances of spectacular violence between Spaniards and islanders, the sickness and privations of the ships' crews, and the crushing failures of their grandiose missions,[28] the well-worn rhetoric of dreamers did not abate. Said Quiros in his famous eighth memorial:

> The lands I saw ... are better than Spain ... [and] should be an earthly paradise.
>
> The day was clear and serene, and as the sun rose over the crowns of the trees, its rays entering through the branches, the difference in the fruits of each plant was shown in great profusion. There, too, could be heard the persistence

with which the birds sang and chaunted; the leaves and
branches were seen to move gently, and the whole place was
agreeable, fresh, shady, with a gentle air moving, and the sea
smooth.

It is a decent people, clean, cheerful, and reasonable, and
as grateful as we have found them. On all these grounds there
is reason to hope that, with the aid of divine providence, and
by gentle means, it will be very easy to pacify, to indoctrinate,
and to content them.[29]

The point need not be labored further. The discovery of the
earthly Pacific paradise and the noble savage by the likes of
Banks and Bougainville some 250 years after Quiros was but a
rerun of a very old Western theme. Even the images did not
originate in the Pacific. Those of us involved in Pacific studies
have tended to be blinkered by disciplinary and geographic
boundaries and have been too impressed with the apparent novelty of the eighteenth-century Pacific dream island. But that
Tahitian mirage was at the end of a very long imaginative tradition, one that long predated the Enlightenment, and even the
Renaissance. Indeed it goes back to the very beginnings of Western civilization. Even in the Pacific context, the predominance
of English perspectives, which tend to focus on the Cook voyages, has until quite recently limited our appreciation of the fact
that for some 300 years before Cook, the Spanish, Portuguese,
and Dutch had explored and offered similar imaginative perceptions of the islands in their search for Terra Australis.[30]

Paradise lost

The Cook voyages heralded the exposure of the hitherto isolated Pacific islands to the wider world. The single most dominant metaphor for the subsequent history of the islands, and
Tahiti in particular as a symbol of all others, is "paradise lost."
Generally this refers to the perceived loss of indigenous innocence and the destruction of island cultures. This is an issue I
will address in chapter 3. Here I offer a different perspective on
the "loss of paradise." In the first place, paradise was lost in the

sense that it was never there. It had not been found in the West
Indies or the Atlantic and Indian Oceans, and it was not in the
Pacific either. Even those who claimed that it was in a particular location, and perhaps believed that it was (and I have quoted
some of them), were not stupid enough not to realize that there
was also some parallel reality—such as violence, perverse sex,
infanticide, cannibalism—that contradicted the image of Eden.
As travelers became more familiar with the Pacific islands,
indeed, even by the time of Cook's second voyage, the earlier
philosophical flights and fancies waned rapidly. The Pacific
islands, and especially Tahiti, were the last possible locations
for an earthly paradise. Since paradise was not there, it was
nowhere on earth. Thus was paradise lost.[31]

But the eighteenth-century Pacific idyll was very short-lived
for other reasons too. There was real physical danger for the
increasing number of outsiders who followed not long after
Cook, not just with the threat of the vast expanse of ocean and
its storms and innumerable fatal reefs, but there was danger
from the inhabitants. Cook was killed in Hawai'i, another paradise, Marion du Fresne was killed in New Zealand, La Pérouse
disappeared forever in Melanesia. As traders and missionaries
followed in Cook's wake, so was begun a long if sporadic history of violent encounter, or at least the outside perception of
violence. By the end of the eighteenth century and right through
the nineteenth century, Westerners commonly regarded the
Pacific with fear and loathing; it was a place of both cultural
and natural dangers.

The nineteenth century was the great imperial age. Newly
discovered regions were assumed ripe for commercial exploitation and political control. The moral and civic imperative was
to impose the unquestioned superiority of Western civilization
on new lands and peoples. That mind-set in itself assumed a jux-
taposition and conflict of opposites—civilization versus savagery
and a tamed, pastoral nature versus an untamed wilderness.
Thus the Pacific islands and their peoples by definition became
that dangerous or unpleasant Other.

In the European consciousness, the noble savage became

the brute savage, a concept greatly intensified by evangelical horror at Pacific societies. The earlier missionaries commonly found in the Pacific islands a beastly wilderness. In spite of the proclaimed triumphs as island after island eventually became "Christianized," the everyday lives of missionaries and especially their wives were fraught with privation, illness, and the constant stress of life amongst cultures they despised. For some, hate turned to fascination and with it sometimes the fall into temptation with island women. For others there was the mixed horror and glory of martyrdom.

Early beachcombers seldom lived up to our retrospectively transferred Romantic myths of an idyllic lifestyle. Most beachcombers in the Pacific islands were escaped convicts from New South Wales or runaways from the harsh realities of shipboard life. Their island experiences in indigenous communities were commonly brutal and certainly traumatic, and most fled as eagerly as they had arrived. Early traders, too, told not of any paradise, but of navigational dangers and fraught relationships with potentially hostile islanders.

Travelers and writers alike tended to emphasize not any Arcadian world, but rather the quirky, the violent, the racial tension, the destruction and dislocation of island cultures, and the moral and physical ruination of both "white men" and islanders in the tropics. The literary account forms a long and illustrious tradition—Edgar Allen Poe, Herman Melville, Robert Louis Stevenson, Paul Gauguin, Jack London, Somerset Maugham, Rupert Brooke.[32] As the century progressed, the Conradian theme that white men were destroyed by the African environment was increasingly echoed in the literature of the Pacific. If anything, the Pacific environment was even more pernicious than the African one in that a Pacific island's apparent beauty could in fact be so cruel. Among the typical if lesser-known examples by the end of the nineteenth–early twentieth century were Louis Becke, who wandered for twenty years around the islands and turned to a demotic accounting in some thirty-five books of white men gone morally and physically astray.[33] "Why indeed, should they leave the land of magical delights for the cold climate and still more glacial moral atmosphere of their native land, miscalled home?" he rhetorically asks.[34] Too late. They have degenerated, become cynical, gone troppo ("The devil!" he has one of his characters say to himself; "I must be turning into a native."[35]). They became more savage than the savage, indulged in gratuitous cruelty and sexual depravity.

> A young girl, at a sign from O'Shea, took off the loose blouse, and they placed her, face downwards, across the bilge of the boat. . . . O'Shea walked round to that side, drawing through his hands the long, heavy, and serrated tail of the *fai*—the gigantic stinging-ray of Oceania. He would have like to wield it himself, but then he would have missed part of his revenge —he could not have seen her face. So he gave it to a native, and watched, with the smile of a fiend, the white back turn black and then into bloody red as it was cut to pieces with the tail of the *fai*.[36]

What was it about the Pacific paradise that led to such moral inversion and collapse? For Becke, a white man "forever dissevered himself from all links and associations of the outside world."[37] And it was not just a physical but a moral disseverement. The Pacific was not only infinitely far from the strictures of civilization. The paradise itself had its own, essentially negative environment, one that with its very beauty and bounty induced a hypnotic paralysis of civilized will and reason: one of his characters still had "fleeting visions of the outside world— that quick, busy world . . . but the calm, placid happiness of his existence, and that strange, fatal glamour that for ever enwraps the minds of those who wander in the islands of the sunlit sea . . . had woven its spell too strongly over his nature to be broken."[38]

Robert James Fletcher, with a degree in chemistry from Oxford, loathed the dulling constraints of English society. Lured to the Pacific in 1912 by Robert Louis Stevenson's writings, Fletcher spent some ten years in the islands, mostly on plantations in the New Hebrides. Letters he wrote to a friend in

England were published in 1923 under the title *Iles of Illusion*. In spite of the physical beauty of coral and palms, Fletcher soon came to loathe the "hideous, mis-shapen, lice-stricken savages," tropical disease, "half-castes, iron houses in the tropic at mid-day, tinned food, scabies, fleas in herds, nerves and jumps." Plantation life was "very nearly hell." He was periodically stricken with malaria. The tropics, he concluded, "are extremely unsuitable as permanent living places for Englishmen." "The sooner I am out of the S. Seas the better... [or] I should have to give free play to the savage that is in me."[39] He recognized the signs of Becke's "fatal glamour": "Unless I am very careful I shall start 'to sleep upon the shore,' and from that sleep there is no awakening."[40] He came to disparage Stevenson for giving him a vision of an ideal South Sea island that was now, in reality, a "shattered dream." "If I had been content with reading Stevenson I should still believe in the paradisaical charm of a coral reef and a coconut tree. Now the one is a thing that stinks like Billingsgate market and knocks nasty holes in expensive boats, while the other is the produce of 1/100th of a ton of copra which also stinks."[41]

Fletcher is actually unfair to Stevenson who, while certainly describing the physical Pacific in glowing images of waving palms and shining sands, and who was himself physically and mentally invigorated for a time there, nevertheless had as a persistent literary undercurrent the potential moral turpitude of white men in the tropics. And Stevenson emphasized the destruction and psychological despair of the islanders once faced with the demands of "civilization."[42]

Distaste of the Pacific can also be found in others who were ostensibly devoted to it. Anthropologist Bronislaw Malinowski, in the depths of Melanesia, revealed his darker thoughts in his diary, referring to the people who hosted him as "nigs" and "brutes." At times he wanted to *"exterminate the brutes,"* a phrase he borrowed from Conrad. He wondered about his more disturbing and often erotic mental meanderings. Were they "because of loneliness and an actual purification of the soul or just tropical madness?"[43] Malinowski neatly captured the contrast between "the picturesque landscape, the poetic quality of the island set on the ocean, and the wretchedness of life here. . . . I would imagine life amid palm groves as a perpetual holiday. That was how it struck me looking from the ship. I had a feeling of joy, freedom, happiness. Yet only a few days of it and I was escaping from it to the company of Thackeray's London snobs."[44] He took refuge in English literature, being particularly fond of Stevenson, Haggard, Kipling, and Conrad.[45]

John Macmillan Brown particularly loathed what he called Rousseau's ideals of a return to a benign nature, though he acknowledged their evil power: "To be wrecked or cast away in the Pacific would not be misfortune, but ejection into paradise."

> What northern boy has not read and re-read *Robinson Crusoe* with its realism and *The Swiss Family Robinson* with its mosaic of impossibilities? Nothing was too absurd for the boyish imagination to accept. . . . The dream lingered, and now and again it came to be realised. . . . And that was chiefly in the South Seas. There is no other region of the tropics that holds in it such possibilities of realising a northen boy's dream.[46]

But the reality, described Brown, was inevitable dereliction. "Lotus-eating . . . in actual working order . . . is the surest prescription for stagnancy, sterility, and racial annihilation. . . . Again and again I met or heard of Europeans . . . some wellborne and well-educated, who had sought this lotus-land, and my impression was that they . . . had fallen to the level of a pig."[47] Brown's Pacific world is characterized by decaying islanders and degenerate, slothful Romantics.

Oceania was thus a wretched place, characterized by danger, poor living conditions, sickness, tropical torpor, degeneration, and sometimes death for white men. We tend to forget that these views, unfashionable as they are now, were predominant for well over a hundred years.

What, I believe, explains this more fundamentally, is not just the Pacific "experience" but a changing Western understanding of nature and a growing appreciation of its power over humans. The perception of the power of nature over culture reached its peak in the nineteenth century. This phenomenon, this understanding of nature's power, this shift in the nature/culture balance, results from a powerful, indeed overwhelming ideological cocktail. I will discuss this much more fully in chapter 2, but here I will just briefly list some of the cocktail's ingredients.

By the end of the eighteenth century there had been a profound change in aesthetic sensibilities. The Burkean notion of the sublime argued that pleasurable pain could come from experiencing wild nature, notably in the mountains and on the sea. And the Romantic movement generally regarded man as part of and subject to the natural world, as opposed to the neoclassical privileging of man over nature.

The development of Enlightenment enquiry coincided with Western discoveries of new natures and new cultures in the New World and the Pacific. What was the essential nature of the "civilized" and the "savage"? What caused the varieties of human societies? Could the "savage" become "civilized"? Could the "civilized" revert to savagery? The formative role of nature/environment/climate became an intense area of study. Montesquieu's notion, stolen from the Greeks, that the climate of Europe produced vigor and intelligence whereas the tropical worlds produced laziness, superstition, weakness, and intellectual stupor underpinned an environmental determinism that featured in the evolving disciplines of moral and racial geography. The claim was that the climate and resources of Europe had produced superior humans and enabled the subordination of nature there, whereas people living outside Europe, particularly in warmer climes, had remained subordinate to nature, which had "worked immense mischief" on their characters and societies. But evolutionary science and its applications to ethnography, anthropology, and psychology of the later nineteenth century stressed the overriding power of *universal* natural laws and the terrifying possibilities for European races moving out of their optimum geographic zone. In the great age of imperial expansion there were profound imperial worries: could European cultures successfully transplant themselves to, and control, distant tropical lands? It was a time of racial fear and of great concern for race survival/improvement. Might not the iron laws of natural selection and the recently appreciated universal capacity for human/cultural degeneration ultimately favor the inferior races, especially the more fecund, such as in Africa? This is not the stuff of paradise, but of nightmares. Paradise was lost in this sense too. Not only had one not been found, but the very idea was now absurd because nature and its iron laws of the "survival of the fittest" would never permit the existence of one.

Paradise regained

Yet paradise was regained. More accurately, the Pacific island paradise has been recreated as a Western cultural site in the twentieth century. How did this come about? My more general explanation is that in the early twentieth century, the nineteenth-century paradigm whereby culture was subservient to nature, and certainly tropical nature, begins to be reversed. Western imperial control, thanks in large part to technological development especially in weaponry and communications, reached its peak in the early twentieth century. This development essentially tamed the indigenous Other and also engendered a sense of control over nature. Chapter 2 will examine this broad idea in detail. What I want to focus on here, in a Pacific context, is the specific example of tourism and how the discourse of tourism deliberately and radically helped to reshape the hostile nineteenth-century image of Oceania.

Tourism for the modern mass market, as opposed to travel for elite social groups, resulted from later-nineteenth-century social and technological change in Western industrial countries. Middle and working classes had more time and money, plus access to transport to indulge in seaside visits, holiday camps, and, eventually, overseas travel.[48] Tourism in the Pacific was certainly dependent on plantation economies, the growth of shipping, undersea cables and then radio waves, and eventually air transport. But even more fundamental was imperial control. By 1900 every Pacific island was formally incorporated into someone's empire and painted the appropriate color on maps. The British in particular gloried in "the Red Route" to and from the Pacific.[49] Thus came a growing sense of psychological control over the Pacific world.

There was a decline of racial fear, provided one had confidence that the firm hand of imperial government was maintained. Beatrice Grimshaw commented: "Fijian civilization is only varnish deep. Cannibalism has been abandoned, cruelty and torture given up, an ample amount of clothing universally adopted, yet the Fijian of 1905, freed from the white control and example that have moulded all his life would spring back like an unstrung bow to the thoughts and ways of his fathers."[50]

Natives themselves are at best loyal, civilized, and Christianized, at worst very much in awe of colonial authority. Even places still remote and potentially dangerous no longer held former terrors. Wandering in New Guinea in the 1920s, an English traveler was startled "to see upon the track before me what looked like a bronze statue armed with a bow and arrows and wearing nothing but a few ornaments. . . . However, I knew that no native would hurt a white man so near to the coast . . . for they have . . . a fear of the white man."[51] A lady visitor to Melanesia in 1915 described how "another Melanesia, sixty years ago, was no Paradise nor yet a land for the tourist . . . [but] in these days of safety . . . the ship anchors quietly and sends a boat ashore certain of welcome."[52]

Tourists were safe from the dangers of "uncontrolled" Pacific societies and any untamed shores. Indeed, not only were most Pacific societies by now regarded as basically tamed, but the indigenous cultures were deemed to be dying out altogether.[53] This near universal belief offered a potential human void in the Pacific. This was to be filled with a new race of Pacific men—the Britons of the south, that is, the European peoples of Australia, and especially New Zealand, who, from the 1880s, regarded themselves as an advanced, reinvigorated

version of their Old World forefathers and represented the
"coming man." John Macmillan Brown was among the more
prominent advocates. "Nature," he proclaimed in the 1920s,
"seems to have marked us out amongst the nations of the great
British Commonwealth as the torchbearers of British civilisation and the British spirit in the Pacific Ocean." New Zealand
had an "Oceanic destiny." It was, said Brown, "in the forefront
of the world and will fully realise the prediction of its epithet
'The Britain of the South.'"[54]

As late as the 1940s, the same arguments could be heard,
though couched in slightly more inclusive terms:

> The culture of the new man ... is more Americo-European
> than anything else. .... The European is strategically placed
> in the Pacific for political, economic and cultural influence. If
> the white peoples of the Americas, of Australia and New
> Zealand follow their interests ... some measure of politico-
> economic union amongst them will appear in the early future;
> and their variety of civilization will control the cultural and
> social formation of the new races.[55]

If there was any potential cultural danger in the Pacific region,
it was now deemed to come from the teeming hordes of Asia.

The early twentieth century saw the climax of depopulation
theory in the Pacific. Anthropologists raced especially to Melanesia to study the last of the doomed islanders. From the start
then, tourists everywhere in the Pacific were fed highly con-
trived images of a pacified, and now wistful, gentle, vanishing
culture. Former "cannibals" and "warriors" were Roman-
ticized as they posed armed but harmlessly for photographs.
Native children became ambivalent objects of innocence, semi-
naked native women objects of male colonial eroticism.[56]

The discourse of early-twentieth-century Pacific tourism
stands in conscious contrast to the nineteenth-century fears
about the dangers of culture and nature in the Pacific. Its fundamental emphasis is on safety. Safe tourism, like safe sex,
requires safe procedures and safe sites. Tourists' visits to Oceania are quick, the return guaranteed. The safest sites are where

colonial political and commercial controls are greatest, and those coincide with regular and reliable shipping and the telegraph cable.

The earliest tourist handbooks and guides to the South Seas, which appeared after the turn of this century, very deliberately tried to counter much of the prevailing mythology about the islands. They emphasized, first, the healthiness of the climate: "The climate of Fiji is probably the healthiest tropical climate in the world, and statistics show that the death rate [for Europeans] is lower than that of the United Kingdom."[57] They also emphasized the strength and stability of colonial government, listing all the political, judicial, and civil institutions and their impressively qualified officeholders. The intention was to create a sense of established "civilization." Next came the safety provided by modern technology. We are told, for example, that "the habits . . . of the natives of the islands may be studied with all the comforts of western civilisation at hand. Steam communications with the outside world is frequent and carried on with modern steamers luxuriantly appointed, in addition to which the All Red Cable, open day and night continuously, permits immediate communication with friends in any quarter of the globe."[58]

Travelers to the Pacific are no longer isolated, no longer removed from home comforts. The copywriters would have you there as cosseted voyeurs, in the region, but not of it. Indeed, the islands are often depicted in familiar, homely images. Vav'au of Tonga is described thus: "the shore for some miles is a succession of bold cliffs, wooded headlands, receding bays, and glistening beaches, with here and there open grassy plots dotted with trees like an English shrubbery."[59] It is reminiscent of early Spanish explorers in the West Indies and the Pacific likening what they saw to Andalusia. Indeed the flights of fancy of the early-twentieth-century tourist copywriters echoed the centuries-old images of the likes of Columbus and Quiros. Here is the Union Steamship Company again, this time talking about Hawai'i: "Here perpetual summer reigns, and the fragrance of

flowers unceasingly fills the air. The wealth of tropical vegetation, the abundance of fruit, the waving palms, the wide acres
of sugar cane, the happy natives, and the sea breaking in long
rolling waves over the coral reefs . . . all these make up a picture
that combine to emphasize the novelty and augment the charms
of this Paradise of the Pacific."[60]

There is also an early physical reenobling of indigenous
populations, especially in Polynesia, and more than a hint of a
dominant colonial male view. The Union Steamship handbook
waxed lyrical about Samoans, for example: "What magnificent
people they are! How handsome with their gold-bronze skins
and yellow hair. . . . The Samoan girls have long been celebrated
for their loveliness and charm, and the traveller is sure to look
with interest on the many graceful feminine forms that pass up
and down the main street of Apia."[61]

Along with cultural safety came a growing sense of ease in
nature. One of the more evocative descriptions comes from a
woman traveler in Fiji in the 1920s. It offers a wonderful coun-
terpoint to the inhibited descriptions by an earlier generation of
Western female visitors:

> Your own toilet next engages your attention. There are no
> bathrooms or wash-bowls in the house; why should there be,
> when Nature has provided a dozen exquisite, shaded pools
> for the bather to choose from? So down to the river you go,
> to slip in to the warm, gently-flowing water that feels so
> smooth and silky to the skin untrammelled by the bathing-
> dress of civilization. Though they add much to your enjoy-
> ment, soap and tooth-brush seem almost sacrilegious in a
> bath fringed with stately, dew-wet tree-ferns and bananas,
> and guarded by hazy, mist-wreathed mountains—a place
> surely designed for elves and fairies rather than for mere
> soapy, mortal man.[62]

So Pacific nature, too, is safe (and sensuous).

This reevaluation of nature is part of a more general earlier-
twentieth-century Western consideration of the nature/culture
balance and a growing sense that nature, rather than being

some unconquerable force, had been tamed both technologically and politically and could indeed be benign, and even restorative. There was a rapid development of outdoor pursuits by middle classes, in part a reaction to growing fears of the possible debilitating consequences of mass urbanization and industrialization. In North America in particular there was an urban-based "back to nature" movement that was "part therapy and part nostalgia." Dozens of early-twentieth-century magazines such as *Rod and Gun* emerged and extolled the possibilities of "ecstasy in non-intellectual adventure" when hunting, fishing, camping in the great outdoors. Nature was increasingly rendered as benevolent mother, capable of reinvigorating a physically deteriorating urban, postfrontier race, and even as a temple where one might find and communicate with deity. Nature, it was increasingly realized, was also in need of protection as well as appreciation.[63] In the Pacific-Australasian context, these ideas were reflected more specifically in sunbathing, swimming in the sea, and the development of beach activities and lifestyles.[64] In turn this related to changing notions of the body, how it might or might not be covered, and how it might be deliberately exposed to the health-giving sun and nature generally. By the mid-twentieth century, the Pacific islands had certainly become a major playground for the recreational sailor, traveler, and tourist, most of whom cavorted in sea and sand and wrote books around the theme of adventures in paradise.

Visual images of the Pacific were transmitted through postcards (with new color technology) and above all by Hollywood. Australian and American filmmakers exploited the expected images of the South Seas from the earliest days of the movies. Alluring island women (generally played by Anglo-Americans), dashing white male heroes, and evil villains acted out fanciful plots of Romantic adventure and treachery set against a backdrop of waving palms and shimmering coral sands.[65] The genre continues, particularly on television.

The physical world of the Pacific has also been recreated according to the idealized images expected by Westerners.

There are numerous modern sites. Some are designed for the mass tourist market and offer what the sociologists of tourism call "pseudo-events" and "staged authenticities," most notably the Polynesian Cultural Center in Hawai'i.[66] After Pearl Harbor it is the most visited location on the island for Hawai'i's thirty million tourists each year. At the Polynesian Cultural Center, Pacific island students from the Brigham Young University act as "natives," climbing coconut trees and rubbing sticks to make fire while being stared at by tourists in canoes paddled along canals that surround the cluster of "islands." It is a Polynesian Disneyland. Similar attractions are Hawai'i's Kodak Hula Show.[67] Club Meds throughout the Pacific also cater to a mass audience in search of a more hedonistic Paradise.

Then there are niche, post-Fordist sites ostensibly offering an authentic and more personalized island experience. Fafa is one of these. But it is no more real than the Kodak Hula Show —only different in scale and focus. It has been carefully created and manicured. It is small, open, landscaped, with coconut palms rising from neatly cut lawns. Deconstructionists might go even further and see it as a female space, the island as a pubic mound, warm, languid in its safe lagoon, as opposed to the high islands elsewhere in the Pacific.[68] Certainly there is no fearful sea or dark jungle hinterland. It is run by a German couple noted for their culinary skills. The island has only twelve *fale*s. There are no crowds, no children, no motor sports. Fafa, like other tourist sites, is in the region, but not of it. Apart from Tongan servants, some local choices on the menu, and a weekly cultural show, it is hardly a "Tongan" experience. But it is the "Pacific" experience that Westerners expect.

Pacific nature has not only become safe and benign this century, but it is also attributed possibilities of refuge, healing, and redemption. Many modern Westerners have sought them, usually unsuccessfully.

Thor Heyerdahl is best known for his *Kon-Tiki* raft expedition from Peru to eastern Polynesia in 1947. But he had visited Polynesia ten years earlier. Was he, as he claimed, the twentieth century's first hippie? The bureaucracy and technology of the modern world had, for Heyerdahl, become a destructive monster. Selecting the Pacific to make his escape, on the basis that "the ocean . . . was so vast that it had neither beginning nor end," he and his new wife ended up on a remote island in the Marquesas. "Back to nature? Farewell to civilization? It is one thing to dream of it and another to do it. I tried it. Tried to return to nature. Crushed my watch between two stones and let my hair and beard grow wild. Climbed the palms for food. Cut all the chains that bound me to the modern world." As they entered the lush valley of Omoa, they likened themselves to Adam and Eve, the difference being that God had driven the original pair out of the Garden of Eden, whereas "we are returning." But the idyllic life living at one with nature soon turned sour. Nature turned out to be too dangerous. Food became scarce, they were plagued by insects and insidious damp and mold, and they ended up sick. They had problems with some of the natives. They fled to other locations in the Marquesas. Eventually it dawned on them. "We are just running away from everything here. It is not what we came to do." "We are just killing time now . . . like the village people, sitting waiting for their coconuts to fall." Clearly there was the danger of physical and intellectual torpor, of *actually* becoming a native. "There is nothing for modern man to return to," Heyerdahl finally admitted; "one can't buy a ticket to Paradise."[69]

The unsuccessful tradition of trying to go back to an idealized nature in the Pacific has continued relentlessly. There are endless examples. In the 1950s and 1960s Tom Neil went to the remote northern Cook Islands: "I chose to live in the Pacific islands because life there moves at the sort of pace which you feel God must have had in mind originally when He made the sun to keep us warm and provided the fruits of the earth for the taking."[70] More recently there was Paul Theroux: "My soul hurt, my heart was damaged, I was lonely. I did not want to see another big city. . . . I wanted to be purified by water and wilderness. . . . The image came to me again, of the Pacific as a universe, and the islands like stars in all that space."[71]

The essence of modern tourism, as opposed to running away to the islands, is that there is no chance of "going native," of being exposed to physical and other dangers, or even of having Romantic dreams of island living dashed. It is all too quick and safe, though still offers the binary contrast of ordinary versus exotic. The introduction of tourist air travel removed the final obstacle of distance and seasickness. Now travelers literally and metaphorically could rise above the island world, to come and go immediately at will, like voyeurs, without engaging in island life for too long. Early tourist aircraft were flying boats with Romantic flying-carpet capabilities, landing in remote lagoons or handy to commercial centers. New Zealand's Tasman Empire Airways Limited commenced its legendary Coral Route from New Zealand to Suva, the Cooks, and Tahiti in 1951.

> Only 6¹/₂ hours [from Auckland] by TEAL Solent to restful Fiji! A short flight in a fast, luxuriously appointed flying boat and there you are. It's so easy by Solent. You land at Lauthala Bay, right in Suva. En route you enjoy all the comforts that have made TEAL Solents famous—fine food service, every attention from Flight Stewards and Stewardesses. Relax in one of Solent's seven lounges as you dream to your winter holiday in restful Fiji.[72]

Akaiami in the Cook Islands was the notable stop, and it frequently took central place in TEAL's promotional literature: "a jewel of an island three kilometres long, with dazzling white sand and coconut palms on the edge of a turquoise lagoon. The warm, shallow water was perfect for swimming or snorkelling, and airline staff thoughtfully handed out togs to passengers who had forgotten to pack their own."[73] TEAL constructed its own jetty there and an "airport building." It was "a native-style thatched hut . . . sited behind the fringe of coconut trees so that it could not be seen from the shore. In this way, the romantic image for the alighting passenger stepping onto an 'unspoilt' Pacific island, was preserved."[74]

Most of us these days travel in jet planes and experience the Pacific in safe, manufactured, and manicured spots, like Waikiki or Fafa. They are Western cultural spaces, not the cultural spaces of the Other to whom they ostensibly belong. Pacific island tourism remains a colonialist activity, not just in social and economic terms, but in its intellectual/imagining processes, even in these so-called postcolonial times. Fafa is not remote and unfamiliar. It is a part of my cultural heritage. Robert Hoskins' postcard presented me with culturally organized information that I already knew and could pleasurably anticipate. Its appeal was far too strong for me to resist. Pacific tourism is not about discovery, it is about confirmation of what we expect to find. I found what I expected on Fafa and came back bearing photographs to confirm the promises of the postcard. Thus the cultural loop is completed.[75]

The modern view of the Pacific as a Westerner's playground paradise, its appeal to secular hedonism, is both ancient and modern. It has no *immediate, direct* links with the neoclassical and politically optimistic and idealistic eighteenth-century version. On the one hand, it goes back far beyond this time, indeed to the earlier days of Western civilization. More especially it is also one filtered and mediated after this time through nineteenth-century dread and recreated and repackaged in the context of the colonial and technical mastery and control of the Pacific islands in the early to mid-twentieth century. The real continuity between old and new paradises in the Pacific lies more in the fact that they remain predicated upon colonialist assumptions and realities and are places wherein nature is reformulated to meet the changing expectations and requirements of Western culture.

Chapter 2

Culture as Nature

THE ASSUMED DISTINCTIONS between the natural/external and the human/social spheres and the relative influences of nature and culture have long been pondered. Clarence Glacken's classic study, *Traces on the Rhodian Shore: Nature and Culture in Western Thought from Ancient Times to the End of the Eighteenth Century,* argued that over this long period no single theory of nature and culture gained ascendancy. Rather a few key ideas flowed in and out of currency, in particular the notion that "the planet was designed for man alone," the idea that "airs, waters and places" influenced cultural characteristics, and, in the latter part of this period, the idea of man as "geographic agent."[1] However, at the point that Glacken's study ends, at the end of the eighteenth century, one can detect the modern beginnings of a view that climaxed in the nineteenth century—the perception that nature was all-powerful over culture, indeed that culture was nature.

The Enlightenment and nature

By Enlightenment times, nature began to be described and given structure by a curiosity-driven, systematic empiricism (notably by Linnaeus), which replaced the emblematic and allegorical treatment of the Renaissance and earlier times.[2] The influences of nature on culture similarly were subject to more complex analysis, even though the basic conclusions were not necessarily all that different from the ancient Greek view. Montesquieu's

Spirit of Laws published in 1748 examined the influence of nature and climate on human sociopolitical and legal organization and in doing so echoed the much older theory of "airs, waters and places" of Hippocrates and Aristotle: "Cold air constringes the extremities of the external fibres of the body; this increases their elasticity, and favors the return of the blood from the extreme parts to the heart. . . . On the contrary, warm air relaxes and lengthens the extremes of the fibres; of course it diminishes their force and elasticity." Thus cold climates produced vigor, boldness, courage, frankness, a sense of superiority and security, though also "little sensibility for pleasure." Hot climates produced faintness, cunning, despondency, incapacity, loss of all vigor and strength, timorousness, though also exquisite sensibility, which meant everything led to the "union of the two sexes." As we move toward warm climates, said Montesquieu, "we fancy ourselves entirely removed from the verge of morality." Heat not only deprived the body of vigor and strength, but "the faintness is communicated to the mind; there is no curiosity, no enterprise. . . . Indolence constitutes the utmost happiness; scarcely any punishment is so severe as mental employment." As a consequence, societies in cold climates could develop rational laws and civic order; in hot countries, despotism and slavery were more likely outcomes.[3]

Throughout the eighteenth century, Enlightenment thinkers debated the relationship between culture and nature: what distinguished man from animals, what explained the differences between the savage and the civilized, what was the essence of moral and civic progress, why did cultures rise and fall? Did "advanced" cultures end inevitably in affluence, ease, sloth, and decay? In particular there was an underlying concern, which was to take the form of real racial fear by the later nineteenth century, that Europeans themselves might degenerate in foreign and especially tropical climes. This remarkable intellectual inquiry coincided with Western awareness of new natures and new cultures in the New World and then the Pacific. Unlike the New World, already much affected by European contact, the

Pacific was seen as an unspoiled, living archive. The discovery of this Other offered unprecedented opportunities for comparative assessments and the testing of hypotheses.[4]

J. R. Forster's *Observations*

One of the earliest and most significant studies of the new Pacific archive was produced by J. R. Forster, the Linnaean scholar taken as naturalist on Cook's second voyage. His *Observations Made during a Voyage Round the World* published in 1778 dealt first with the "physical and natural history" of the islands and the ocean. Two-thirds of the treatise, though, was devoted to "the human species," a complex account of the size, varieties, and nature of island societies.[5] Forster was not just interested in these societies per se but in what they might add to an understanding of humankind more generally. Forster believed that societies developed like human individuals. Infancy he likened to animalism, childhood to savagery, adolescence with its fiery passion to barbarism, adulthood and maturity to civilization. He placed Pacific societies in the childhood/savagery category. But he was puzzled how within such a category there were so many varieties of cultures. For some comparisons, his deliberate application of the climatic determinism of Montesquieu seemed to work. For example, warm, luxuriant Tahiti, which he regarded as "the queen of tropical societies," ranked higher on the scale of happiness than temperate New Zealand, which in turn had far happier inhabitants than the miserable wretches of frozen Terra del Fuego. But what about societies that differed within the same climatic zone, such as the happy, pleasant Tahitians and the unhappy, nasty Malekulans? Here Forster sought cultural explanations. Accepting the common belief in monogenesis, Forster argued that "all the improvements of mankind . . . ought to be considered as *the sum total of the efforts of mankind ever since its existence.*"[6] Thus societies that maintained the "principles of education," those that increased and passed on knowledge, improved, while others

degenerated. Dissimilar societies in similar climates perhaps
had had different historical experiences and had become different people in times past. In this case, he suggested, the islands
were settled by separate migrations.

Forster's division of Pacific island peoples into two broad
categories that much later would be given by others the names
Melanesian and Polynesian and his gradation of Pacific societies into a hierarchical scheme helped to establish a framework
of Pacific anthropological discourse that has lasted virtually to
the present. But his findings also had wider application. Johann
Friedrich Blumenbach, for example, who drew up a hierarchy
for all human societies, with Caucasians obviously at the top,
included Pacific islanders in his Malays category after reading
Forster.[7] Alexander von Humboldt acknowledged his debt to
J. R. Forster and especially to his son Johann George, who had
accompanied his father on Cook's voyage and had written his
own account. He also translated his father's work into German.
Humboldt declared that the Forsters had "prompted me to
undertake distant travels."[8] He was particularly impressed with
their finding on differences and similarities of various climatic
zones and their privileging of the denseness and diversity of
flora and fauna in tropical climates over the allegedly poorer
life forms in frozen regions. Humboldt was later to find his
tropical inspiration in South America.

Forster's work deserves highlighting not just because it has
largely been unappreciated, but because Forster's *Observations*
marks a significant moment wherein theory and empirical data
do not quite mesh. The one has the capacity to modify the
other. Forster saw a complex relationship between culture and
nature, both having a bearing on the type and character of a
society. In this way, Forster's empirical observations supported
and also challenged aspects of prevailing theories about the
conditions of humanity. The simple hot/cold dichotomy of
Montesquieu was not sufficient on its own to explain differences: "though the climate greatly influences the happiness of a
nation," said Forster, "it is however not the only cause of its

real felicity; that education contributes as much, if not more, towards the good state of the people; and that the removal from the tropics towards the colder extremities of the globe, together with the gradual loss of the principles of education greatly contribute to the degeneracy and debasement of a nation into a low and forlorn condition."[9]

But the experience of observation together with the appreciation of complexity that characterized J. R. Forster's work was often to be far less marked by many others who came after him, in the nineteenth century. Moreover, Forster's Enlightenment ethnocentrism was a rather more muted phenomenon than the strident racism of the nineteenth century.

As indicated in the previous chapter, by the end of the eighteenth century there was already a fairly stiff aesthetic and ideological cocktail of the Burkean sublime and Romanticism generally; it stressed that man was both a part of and subject to the forces of nature. For much of the nineteenth century, and into the early twentieth, observation, if it occurred, was often used to support, rather than question, the increasingly pervasive and *racially* informed opinion that culture was overdetermined by nature. To illustrate this generalization, I will arbitrarily and artificially delineate two broad disciplinary strands, environmental determinism and ethnography/anthropology.

Environmental determinism

The major figures in the development of the discipline of geography in the late eighteenth and early nineteenth century entrenched the idea that different environments helped to explain, if not totally determine, different cultural customs and characters.[10] A key aspect of Immanuel Kant's philosophy was physical geography. Kant believed that knowledge came either from pure reason or through the senses. Sense perception could be inner (the soul), or outer (nature). Physical geography studied nature, and such study was basic to an understanding of how humans perceived the world and of how the natural world had influenced humans. Natural laws influenced humans, since humans were part of nature. Physical geography was the basis for other geographies suggested by Kant, such as mathematical, moral, political, commercial, theological. But Kant was no environmental determinist. Through human reason, humans could transcend and alter their lot. Karl Ritter and Alexander von Humboldt were very much influenced by Kant's Idealism and variously stressed the overall unity and harmony of organic nature, of which man was a part—"one great whole animated by the breath of life."[11] But it was a unity in diversity. Thus systematic, comparative study was required, but it had to move beyond simply description and classification and seek relationships, or "causal connection." For Humboldt, organic life could not adequately be described by classificatory systems. It needed to be understood in its respective "zones of habitation," according to latitude, elevation, and climatic influences. "The manners and institutions . . . [and] feelings" of humans similarly were influenced by their respective zones of habitation: "this character of *geographical individuality* attains its maximum . . . in countries where the differences in the configuration of the soil are the greatest possible, either in vertical or horizontal direction, both in relief and in the articulation of the continent."[12]

If various plants had certain optimum locations, might not various people also have their proper place? This idea, combined with evolutionary thinking from the mid-nineteenth century and related Victorian racial typology, soon saw a vigorous *racial* geography. An early version was Henry Thomas Buckle's *History of Civilisation in England* (1857–1861), which claimed to establish two facts that are the "necessary basis of universal history":

> in the civilisations out of Europe, the powers of Nature have been far greater than in those in Europe. The second fact is, that those powers have worked immense mischief. . . . Hence it is that looking at the history of the world as a whole, the

tendency has been, in Europe, to subordinate nature to man; out of Europe to subordinate man to nature.[13]

It thus followed, said Buckle, that to study the histories of countries outside Europe you had to study their natural environment, but to study the history of countries within Europe you could make "man our principle study." Here is the clear linking of the non-European Other with nature and all the related connotations of that Other therefore being lesser, primeval, primitive, animalistic, and an available specimen. Also, for Buckle and others, ultimately it was nature, not man, that determined which races would flourish. Only where nature was weak was it possible to increase "the dominion of the human mind over the agencies of the external world."[14]

As Darwinian/Lamarckian influences increased their intellectual and emotional grip from midcentury, the analysis became even more bleak. Notably there was now a very clear break from earlier views of the nature of nature itself. Nature no longer occupied a spectrum from the Arcadian/Edenic through to the sublime. It was now a universal and essentially malevolent force—ranging from weak to strong. Gone was the idealism of unity and simple locational and static variation in nature. Nature was now pitiless, driven by a dynamic that postulates only struggle. The added element of chance suggested that there was no certainty, *anywhere,* that "civilized" peoples might remain in control. "Nature," said Freud, "is sublime, pitiless, inexorable thus bringing to mind our weaknesses and helplessness, of which we thought the work of civilisation had rid us."[15]

One obvious consequence of this was to re-invent serious doubts about whether Europeans, for all their superior rationality and vigor, could survive in foreign and especially tropical climates. This idea was actually a very old one, originating in medieval notions that humans could inhabit neither "frigid" polar regions nor "torrid" equatorial zones. Once that was disproved, the idea of European degeneracy when living outside temperate regions remained a critical concern. Lord Kames had asked James Lind, who was about to go on Cook's second expedition, to investigate the question, "Are not men, like horses or wheat, apt to degenerate in foreign climes?" Questions like these, said Kames, lead

> to a deep speculation viz what is the scheme of providence for peopling the earth with the human race. Abstracting from Revelation it is natural to conjecture, that as there are many different climates, there were formed originally different races of men fit for these different climates, in which only they flourish and degenerate in every other climate.[16]

There was an even deeper set of fears, which had also been around at least since the Enlightenment, that degeneration even while staying at home was a possibility. Civilization itself might lead to ease, indulgence, and demise, while other civilizations might arise. It had long been common to speculate on the possibility that the British might be eclipsed by the rise of civilization among the natives of the Antipodes and Oceania: "when New Zealand may produce her Lockes, her Newtons, and her Montesquieus; and when the great nations in the immense region of New Holland, may send their navigators, philosophers, and antiquaries, to contemplate the ruins of *ancient* London and Paris, and to trace the languid remains of the arts and sciences in this quarter of the globe."[17] Dumont D'Urville expressed similar sentiments,[18] all of which foreshadowed T. B. Macaulay's 1840 vision of a Maori standing on the remains of London Bridge sketching the ruins of St. Paul's.

Fears of European degeneracy, hardened by a savage evolutionism, often were a feature of general social theory across the second half of the nineteenth century. Apparent increases in criminality, insanity, suicide, drunkenness, pornography, and degenerative illnesses, combined with declining birth rates, created various "national" anxieties. Degeneracy was not just individual, but collective. Conservatives and liberals could justify their fear of socialism in terms of the latent "natural" power of merciless mobs:

> We must remember that, however much society at large may
> have changed for the better, the lowest stratum of all has not
> changed, and that lawlessness, cupidity, and ruffianism are
> just as rife now as they were in the days of Sir Robert Walpole
> or Lord George Gordon. We see by what a very thin and pre-
> carious partition after all are we divided from the elements of
> violence which underlies all civilized societies.[19]

The basis for such observations was not just a "Victorian"
moralizing, but a sustained and well-developed medical model
enmeshed in evolutionary, racial, and environmental concepts.
Subverting the ideals of civilization and decency were the potentially more powerful forces of biological and mental degeneracy, a product, at least in part, of adaptation to an urban and
industrial environment. Recent scholarship has suggested that if
"medicine has a political and cultural history . . . so do politics
and culture have a medical history."[20]

If it was dangerous at home, it was vastly more so in the
tropics. By later Victorian times, the fear of white men morally
as well as physically degenerating in the tropics was a key concern, exemplified in the works of Conrad. As empire expanded,
notions of the tropics as "the white man's grave" developed.[21]
New medical literature highlighted the terrible dangers. Apart
from death from diseases, there were theories about the dangers
of tropical light itself, which, some argued, was positively dangerous to white men, producing the condition of "neurasthe-
nia" or "tropical amnesia."[22] It was widely believed that Europeans would never be able to control their empires properly
because of the "innate unnaturalness of the whole idea of
acclimatization in the tropics, and of every attempt arising out
of it to reverse by an effort within human range the long, slow
process of evolution which has produced such a dividing line
between the inhabitants of the tropics and those of temperate
regions."[23] Ironically, then, there were serious questions about
biological and racial security at the very moment of unprecedented imperial expansion into tropical zones, and especially
the "dark" continent of Africa with its assumed heat, jungles,

disease, and ferocious animals and peoples. But as indicated in the previous chapter, the dangers were no less in the Pacific, and indeed they were probably more insidious and subtle given the apparent physical beauty of the islands.

A moralistic geographic determinism lasted well into the twentieth century. The 1920s and 1930s especially saw a huge literature on racial geography and relationships between climate and civilization.[24] Ellsworth Huntington was a notable contributor. "For every species of living being," he claimed, "there seems to be a certain optimum or most favourable condition." For humans, greatest health and energy were produced in regions when the average day and night temperature was 60–68 degrees F. Thus Nordic peoples of northwest Europe "possess an innate tendency toward unusual activity, boldness, self-reliance, initiative and other allied traits." Peoples living in different climatic zones were likely to be dull and stupid. "Temperatures that are too high have a worse effect than those that are too low." Over time, the brains of races became differentiated. Huntington constructed a remarkable series of "climographs" and attempted to demonstrate that the relationship between "climatic energy" and "civilisation" is "almost identical."[25] As late as 1939, Grenfell Price, in his study *White Settlers in the Tropics,* basically agreed with Huntington that "climatic and social statistics tend to support the evidence of history, which indicates that tropical conditions make human settlement and the evolution of a high standard of civilization extremely difficult."[26]

Ethnography/anthropology

The history of ethnographic and anthropological thought from Enlightenment times through the nineteenth century generally emphasizes changes in approach and methodology—from Enlightenment classicism, to early-nineteenth-century scriptural interpretation, to mid-nineteenth-century comparative science, and its subsequent overlay of evolutionism. But what is sometimes underestimated in this narrative are a number of unchanging assumptions during this period, and beyond. One was the notion of monogenesis—the idea of a common human origin. Another was the assumption about the possibilities of progression through the gradations of hunting, pastoral, agricultural, and industrial, or of regression and degeneration.[27] As mentioned earlier, Pacific island societies were considered as valuable specimens of the earlier stages of human development. It is worth emphasizing that ideas of and fears about human cultural mutability, whether the explanation be cultural or environmental, long predated Darwinian thought. Darwinism, and so-called Social Darwinism, both of which were actually more Lamarckian than strictly Darwinist at the time,[28] further entrenched that idea.

Evolutionary thought thus easily and readily wove itself into the centrality of ethnography and anthropology. Later-nineteenth-century texts on the nature of civilization, on the relationship of the savage and the civilized, and on the dynamics of moving between the two stressed the immutable, universal laws of a remorseless nature in explaining human cultural as well as biological characteristics. More than this, history itself was determined by these natural laws. History was evolution. Edward Tylor, commonly regarded as the founding father of modern anthropology, argued in his *Primitive Culture* (1871) that human history was "part and parcel of the history of nature, that our thoughts, wills, and actions accord with laws as definite as those which govern the motion of waves, the combinations of acids and bases, and the growth of plants and animals." And the laws of nature also determined the course of culture—"a movement along a measured line from grade to grade of actual savagery, barbarism and civilisation."[29] To quote Derek Freeman, "Evolutionism and monistic theory thus dealt with the age-old question of the relationship between culture and nature by pronouncing that culture was an entirely natural process, like the growth of plants and animals, and not to be differentiated from other natural phenomena."[30] This notion was taken to extremes by the early twentieth century.

Francis Galton, for example, argued that biological Darwinism could also be applied to human moral and mental capacities. Thus differences between the savage and the civilized could be explained by the "innate character of different races."[31] Galton founded the eugenics movement, which was devoted to race improvement by advocating selective breeding to control and improve human biological and mental evolution.

Depopulation

The importance of the Pacific islands as a laboratory in the development of geographic and anthropological thought cannot be overstated. Not only were there numerous Western scientific expeditions to the Pacific, but throughout the nineteenth century, Pacific-based missionaries, administrators, and scholars both applied the anthropological fashions of the time and published their own findings and also sent vast amounts of information about island cultures back to the greats of European and especially British anthropology—such as Darwin, Friedrich Max Müller, J. G. Frazer, and Tylor—who included this information in their seminal works.[32] And just as the Pacific was a major laboratory for human studies, it remained one of the single most important laboratories for the natural sciences. Investigations of the nature of icebergs and coral reefs and into the distribution, boundaries, and variety of plants and animals led directly to evolutionary theory.[33] Darwin himself came to his understanding of natural selection while on the *Beagle*'s voyage in the Pacific. Islands in the Pacific, and elsewhere, have subsequently been the proving ground for natural selection and for an understanding of its complex operations right through to the present. Robert MacArthur's *Theory of Island Biogeography* (1967) finally "brought the island biogeography paradigm to the mainlands."[34]

The interpretation of Pacific islands cultures through the nineteenth century and into the twentieth directly reflected, and helped to support, the hardening analysis of environmental determinism and anthropological/ethnographic moralizing. Opinions about Pacific islanders varied over this time, ranging from eighteenth-century neoclassicists' noble savages, to the early-nineteenth-century missionaries' brutish savages, to mid- to later-nineteenth-century theorists' Romantic or dying savages. Theories of origins also varied, from classical Mediterranean, to Semitic, to Aryan.[35] But some initial and constant assumptions need stressing. One was that Pacific islanders belonged to the single, original family of humankind, but had become separated and degenerated over the ages as they wandered the earth and ended up on the islands of the Pacific. This notion of degeneracy is a critical one. It underlies eighteenth-century and later Western assumptions of the inherent inferiority and passivity of Pacific cultures, *and* of their fundamental fragility. These perceived weaknesses were deemed aggravated by the smallness of populations (there were no teeming hordes) and their isolation on the tiniest of homelands. And then there were the debilitating mental and other consequences of their respective tropical oceanic environments, which either were directly damaging or more subtlety destructive by inducing a pleasurable sloth that led to physical and moral decay.

If it was widely believed that Europeans could not survive in the tropical islands, the analysis was even more bleak for the indigenous inhabitants, and indeed, as I will suggest in the next chapter, this discouraging view may reflect a projection of Western fears for itself onto unsuspecting islanders.

The notion that Pacific islanders were either doomed before Europeans arrived or were doomed by that arrival is based on an assumption of the fundamental moral and biological weaknesses of islanders. Because of the way in which they had been molded by nature, they were assumed to be fatally flawed.

Even at the time of the Cook voyages, there was an expectation that island cultures were destined for disaster with the arrival of all-powerful, restless "civilization." As Cook himself moralized, "We debauch their Morals already too prone to vice and we interduce among them wants and perhaps diseases which they never before knew and which serves only to disturb that happy tranquillity they and their fore Fathers had injoy'd."[36] This sentiment, widely echoed, was no better expressed than by George Forster on Cook's second voyage:

> It were indeed sincerely to be wished, that intercourse which has lately subsisted between Europeans and the natives of the South Sea islands may be broken off in time, before the corruption of manners which unhappily characterizes civilized regions, may reach that innocent race of men, who live fortunate in their ignorance and simplicity.[37]

The idea of a "fatal impact" is perhaps the single most dominant trope in the historiography of the Pacific islands,[38] and, as already indicated, it generally set the stage for the idea of the Pacific paradise lost. Thus the noble savage purists lamented the destructive capacities of "civilization" and argued the case for leaving the Pacific alone. Missionaries who specifically wanted to impose a beneficent "civilization" upon islanders conceded that the darker aspects of Western contact, such as vice, booze, and general debauchery, were destroying them. In turn missionaries themselves were blamed for stultifying and ruining formerly vibrant cultures with their oppressive moralities. The argument about what was causing the destruction of Polynesia raged throughout the first half of the nineteenth century, but there was no argument about the final expected result: "There seems to be a certain incompatibility between the tastes of the savage and the pursuits of civilized man, which, by a process more easily marked then explained, leads in the end to the extinction of the former; and nowhere has this shown itself more visibly than in Polynesia."[39]

These thoughts predated Darwinism, which did not, in itself, introduce any dramatic new ideas into Pacific studies. Rather it reinforced pervasive Christian notions of degeneration and demise. And it was quite compatible with notions of ascending and descending human types and societies that featured in the pre-Darwinian comparative scientific works of

Max Müller and Edward Tylor that had so influenced Polynesian studies to that point. Evolutionary thought over the second half of the nineteenth century both confirmed the process of extinction and provided "scientific" explanation. Pacific islanders "have long been doomed, in obedience ... to immutable laws, to extinction. Of late, they are marching more rapidly to their destined goal, and no mortal hand can stay their fatal progress. But this is no matter for fond regrets or philanthropic sighs. These Polynesian have doubtless performed some allotted part in the economy of nature."[40] The more philosophically inclined saw the extinction of the Polynesian peoples as an opportunity for "the great English nation ... [to] learn from their varied career the transitory nature of human greatness."[41] Not only was evolutionary thinking applied to the Pacific, but the Pacific was a proving ground for the veracity of the theory. One immediate consequence was an attempt at salvage ethnography. Percy Smith made a hasty trip to the islands in 1897:

> Time was pressing—the old men of the Polynesian race from whom their history could be obtained were fast passing away —civilization was fast extinguishing what little remained of ancient lore—the people themselves were dying out before the incoming white man—and, to all appearances, there would soon be nothing left but regrets over lost opportunities.[42]

Within the assumed evolutionary dynamic there continued to be argument about the specific mechanic or agency of extinction: was it disease, alcohol, firearms, European clothing and diets, repressive controls and regulations? Stevenson did much to popularize what he called the "psychological factor."

> The Polynesian falls easily into despondency ... and sadness detaches him from life. ... With the decay of pleasures, life itself decays. ... Each change, however small, augments the sum of new conditions to which the race has become inured. ... The unaccustomed race will sometimes die of pin-pricks. ... Experience seems to show us (at least in Polynesian

islands) that change of habit is bloodier than a bombard-
ment.[43]

The literature on the imminent extinction of Pacific islanders reached its peak in the 1920s.[44] A good deal of it continued
to echo later-nineteenth-century views. Many commentators
emphasized the argument that racial extinction would have
happened even without Western entry. S. H. Roberts claimed
that the islanders' world, denied "the health-giving process of
selection and of struggle," was "rotting to the core" before
Europeans arrived.[45] John Macmillan Brown explained how
once the peoples of Polynesia had given up voyaging in search
of new homes they succumbed to the temptations of their tropical environment. Warmth and fertility meant that

> the necessity for strenuous work has passed over them; the
> curse of the idle and luxurious falls upon them, the doom of
> race sterility. . . . Work is the only antiseptic for races or
> nations. And where Nature is left to herself she makes sure
> that her children will not cease to use that medicament. If she
> wishes to destroy a section of mankind she takes care that
> they will have a good time and adopt as their ideal that all
> must have a good time.[46]

Thus, according to Brown, the racial heart had given out on
Pacific islanders, and their extinction was assured, long before
Europeans arrived.

The revival of the idea of culture

By about the beginning of the twentieth century, when the privileging of nature over culture—the idea that culture essentially
was nature—was at its peak, a counteroffensive began. Subsequently we have witnessed the development of the notion that
culture is more independent of nature and more able to determine itself. This shift can in part be traced to changes within the
disciplinary streams examined earlier; it is also related to the

actuality of colonial political and economic controls and the associated sense of control over nature.

Geographic environmental determinism eventually had its opponents, who advocated a "possibilism," a return to a neo-Kantian Idealism that allowed for human reason, ethics, and action to influence the fate of societies and cultures.[47] This possibilism was also reflected in anthropology in at least two respects. There was a gradual rethinking or redefining of the bases upon which a society was deemed "primitive": was it simply the presence or absence of certain knowledge and the development of a functional efficiency within a certain environment, or was it more fundamentally innate? Also there was the rise of a cultural or social determinism that specifically challenged an environmental or natural determinism. Pacific islands case studies were pivotal in these developments.

In 1898, A. C. Haddon led a team of Cambridge anthropologists, which included W. H. R. Rivers and C. G. Seligman, to the Torres Strait.[48] They conducted a series of psychological tests, such as responses to stimuli and color recognition, with a view to determining how and why a "primitive" society differed from a "modern" one. Their conclusions seriously challenged the assumption of most nineteenth-century anthropology that primitive societies represented various earlier stages of development of modern Westerners. The perceptual skills of so-called primitive minds, the Cambridge anthropologists argued, differed from that of their own only by virtue of being products of a different environment. Rivers commented that the study of primitive psychological processes "leads us into no mystical dawn of the human mind, but introduces us to concepts and beliefs of the same order as those which direct our own activities."[49] The difference between the savage and the civilized, then, was no longer considered one of evolutionary distance, but merely one of different social and physical environments.[50] But there was still the problem of how those respective environments actually influenced culture. Most eugenicists, for example, emphasized the inheritance of mental characteristics, whereas the nascent cultural determinists favored the socializing processes.

And so the nature/culture debate, or, as it was called, the nature/nurture debate, was rekindled. Franz Boas, who championed the cause of cultural determinism, had one of his young students go to Samoa for fieldwork in the 1920s. Her conclusions, that nurture—in this case communal, loving, free, easygoing, and sexually permissive—explained why Samoan youths had none of the problems of American "teenagers," who were instead burdened with repressive, moralistic conventions. Teenage trauma, said Margaret Mead, was a problem of culture, not of nature. Mead's *Coming of Age in Samoa* not only became perhaps *the* anthropological classic of the twentieth century,[51] but helped to set assumptions and an agenda for American anthropology that only recently have been challenged. Derek Freeman has exposed Mead's prejudgments and her being told a series of tall sexual tales by a small group of Christian Samoan girls whom she interviewed.[52] But the point to be made here is that Mead's case study of Samoa, regardless of its methodological shortcomings, is a foundational part of the process whereby an anthropological cultural determinism eventually gained the ascendancy within the discipline. The rejection of naturalist and evolutionary influences in interpretations of human social behavior has been a basis for most subsequent history and anthropology.

Other equally profound though now much less celebrated examples in Pacific anthropological theory and practice helped to strengthen the case for culture. Early-twentieth-century anthropologists generally believed that most indigenous Pacific peoples were culturally dislocated and dying out. The race was on particularly to find and study cultures as yet "untainted" by European contact. The best subjects for such salvage anthropology were thought to be the peoples of Melanesia, on the rather naive assumption that Melanesian communities had

experienced less contact with Europeans than those of Polynesia. The anthropologists who turned up there were among
the first generation of "professional" anthropologists. They
believed in the necessity of fieldwork, as opposed to the arm-
chair techniques of their "amateur" forebears. Perhaps a parallel might be drawn here with the Cook voyages, a similar
moment when observation and local experience had the capacity to confound at least aspects of abstract speculation. But it
was going to be touch and go. As Malinowski wrote, "Just
now, when the methods and aims of scientific field ethnology
have taken shape, and when men fully trained for the work have
begun to travel into savage countries and study their inhabitants—these die away under our very eyes." But Malinowski
and others did manage to find inhabited islands. And the interplay of observation and theory was indeed complex.

One critical result was the emergence of anthropological
functionalism. It had its early intellectual roots with the 1898
Cambridge expedition. Haddon, Rivers, Seligman, and William
McDougall not only made major contributions to British
anthropology, often using Melanesian and southwest Pacific
case studies, but "spawned distinguished lines of professorial
descendants"—notably A. R. Radcliffe-Brown and Bronislaw
Malinowski with his *Argonauts of the Western Pacific*,[53] who
were generally acknowledged as the fathers of functionalism,
which came of intellectual age in the 1920s and 1930s. Much
modern British anthropology essentially cut its teeth in early-
twentieth-century Melanesia. That scene moved to Africa from
the 1930s, since fieldwork was cheaper there.[54]

Functionalism, which was generally applied to non-
European societies, argued that a culture consisted of various
operating compartments—political, religious, economic, sexual, psychological, and so on. Their successful individual and
collective workings assured the survival of the society. But the
logic of functionalism meant, first, that these societies were
regarded as fairly static. That is, they had reached a kind of

functional equilibrium in their environment. Change really only came about by the introduction of ideas and technologies from outside—the notion of diffusionism. Second, they were seen as inherently fragile, in that change in any one compartment was likely to upset the rest. F. E. Williams, government anthropologist for Papua from the 1920s, adopted his "scandalous simile," likening indigenous cultures to a "pile of rubbish. Poke it with a stick, add or remove one empty jam-tin, and, however slight the change, you have affected the whole mass, through and through. Remove, let us say from its midst, a thing so great as an empty kerosene-tin, and you may create a disturbance of almost volcanic proportions."[55] Thus early-twentieth-century anthropology was keen to describe indigenous societies in their assumed static, pristine, pre-contact forms. Social change in itself was not deemed a fashionable subject for anthropological study. Rather, social change in indigenous societies, especially after European contact, was more likely to be lamented as a sign of decay. In this sense, functionalism contributed notably to the general sense of culture crisis for Pacific societies as a result of Western contact. Not surprisingly, as already mentioned, anthropologists were fervent believers in the phenomenon of Pacific islands depopulation. However, their explanations tended to be different from some. Where the finger was commonly pointed at disease, or alcohol, or commerce, or Christianity, early-twentieth-century anthropologists, while admitting some or all of these agents, tended to favor Stevenson's psychological factor. A changed way of life, whatever its actual cause, could induce a paralyzing despair, a loss of collective will. Said Rivers, "I believe . . . [the] first and foremost among the causes of the dying out of the Melanesian . . . [is] the loss of interest in life from which at present he is suffering."[56]

Yet there was a major irony here. Functionalism, by its very definition, highlighted the importance of culture, and hence the possibilities of culture. Culture was not, as others might claim, dictated to by a relentless nature. Culture, its functional components, might be influenced by "good," such as medicine, housing, and education, as well as by the "evils" of disease, alcohol, cross-cultural contact, and the like. In other words, perhaps there were cultural solutions to problems such as depopulation, as opposed to a neo-Darwinian acceptance of its inevitability. Not only might there be cultural solutions, but now the problems themselves were more likely deemed cultural as well; hence the focus was just as much on the psychological consequences of change as on the agents of change per se. Rivers, for example, stressed the importance of detailed studies of custom in Melanesia to see what was crucial to cultural well-being and what was not. The blanket disapproval of all native custom, a common enough response in the nineteenth century, especially by many missionaries, had, said Rivers, done great damage: "this unintelligent and undiscriminating action towards native institutions . . . [meant] the people were deprived of nearly all that gave interest to their lives" and resulted in psychological despair. Rivers pondered the possibilities of gentle cultural manipulation and substitution. Might it have been possible, he mused, to have modified rather than repressed the practice of headhunting in the Solomon Islands? Rivers regarded headhunting as wrong. It had to be stopped. But what was its "inner meaning"? He thought there were two aspects. The taking of heads was an ancient human sacrificial practice. Thus it performed a ceremonial function. It also generated a vigorous canoe-making industry—an economic function. So perhaps the Solomon Islanders might have been persuaded to substitute pigs' heads for human ones, thereby maintaining the ceremonial connection, and to replace the raiding voyages with organized canoe racing, thereby retaining the economic motives.[57]

Early-twentieth-century anthropologists advocated what they believed to be a sensitive, scientifically based intervention in indigenous life, one based on a sound anthropological understanding of that life. But anthropological science was never neutral or value-free. It was very much part of the broader context of colonial paternalism. In addition to highlighting the role of anthropology in my argument about the shifting balance of

nature to culture, it is necessary to emphasize the fact of colonial rule, and the assumed conquest of nature in the early twentieth century—and all this involved notions of destiny.

Destiny

Most Pacific islanders had formally been incorporated into the
various empires of the Western nations by the turn of the twentieth century. British colonial administrators seemed more concerned than most with the perceived problem of depopulation,
mainly because Britain (together with Australia and New Zealand) was the predominant colonial ruler in the southwestern
Pacific, where the issue of depopulation tended to be focused.
Although some frankly applauded the imminent extinction of
island societies, colonial officials were less likely to take this
line for two main reasons. First, the annexation of islands often
had been justified on humanitarian grounds, promising protection to the indigenous inhabitants. For example, the British
annexation of Fiji in 1874, and indeed the earlier annexation of
New Zealand, was ostensibly to save their inhabitants from the
damaging consequences of unregulated European presence. The
doctrine of the "white man's burden" was an essential ingredient of ideologies of imperial destiny in the Pacific. Any arguments that great nations were at the mercy of immutable natural laws were challenged:

> The future of Polynesia is a British responsibility. Our sons
> and daughters have made Australasia a great dominion and
> their children will assuredly fulfil the destiny of the Anglo-
> Saxon race in ultimately ruling most of the islands between
> the City of the Golden Gate and New Zealand. . . . The races
> now inhabiting the islands of the South Pacific are worthy of
> our care.[58]

Second, the disappearance of an indigenous population,
particularly in the tropical Pacific where there was no prospect
of large-scale colonial settlement, was clearly a massive economic waste. As one commentator said, "Apart from all con-

siderations of humanity, it is to the advantage of the Government to save the native race. These [Melanesian] islands without a population are entirely useless."[59]

> The history of the Pacific, and especially of the Polynesians, shows us a people who have degenerated from a noble race in the past, *and who may be regenerated again,* for it is in our hands to do so. There is nothing more harmful, nothing more weak and criminal, than the canting cry: "The Pacific Islanders are dying out; what is the use of bothering?" *They need not die out....* No, *if the natives are given their chance* they can increase, and can be made good and useful citizens—an asset to the Empire—and the matter lies in our hands.[60]

The question was, of course, how to do it. The issue had been highlighted by the 1893 Fijian commission to "inquire into the Decrease of the Native Population." Its recommendations were for a comprehensive and heavy-handed intervention by government into almost every aspect of indigenous life. Early-twentieth-century colonial rule often carried with it a commitment to bring about fundamental social engineering. Administrative and anthropological theory shared a common assimilationist goal, based on the premise that the problems in question were ultimately cultural in origin and that therefore there were cultural solutions. Differences between administrative goals and the policies advocated by anthropologists differed in degree rather than kind. And indeed, by the 1920s and 1930s there were close institutional and training links between government and anthropology. Colonial administrators were commonly instructed by anthropologists. Anthropology was more consciously than ever an integral part of the colonizing processes. More than this, anthropology determined interpretation of culture for purposes of government. In an ironic sense, there was a return to Forster's ideas of the "principles of education"—the notion that Pacific societies had lost their intellectual way, had degenerated, and now required instruction in how to adapt to modernity. To be successful, such instruction needed to take account of their long, different, and essentially unhappy histories and cultures. Such anthropological insight, it was argued, would reduce the islanders' obstacles and opposition to the required radical change; "enlightening imperial self-interest . . . would reduce its weight, not only for the English, but for the savage."[61]

As indicated in chapter 1, the effective imposition of colonial rule in the Pacific, and related ideas of racial imperial destiny, also led to a growing sense of Western control over nature in the region. Indeed one might think more globally and see the early twentieth century as a time when a Western hegemony appeared to be established over most of the world. It was a time when it was claimed nature had been tamed. Great rivers had been diverted and dammed. Isthmuses were cut open and seas joined. Tunnels pierced mountains. Railways went everywhere. Great forests were cleared, great swamps drained. Telegraph cables then radio waves encircled the globe. Both regional and international geographic frontiers were essentially at an end. The poles were reached. Slocum sailed single-handed around the world. The Pacific islands in particular were now seen as a safe playground for recreational sailors, travelers, tourists. The Western body in nature was redefined. Nature itself could be redemptive. The island paradise was recreated. And in the 1930s, even the problem of depopulation was considered solved. Island populations appeared to be increasing, and the increase was invariably explained in terms of colonial government initiatives in health, housing, education. Relocation schemes had to be implemented for some of the more crowded atolls. It was the high noon of Pacific colonialism. There was a self-congratulatory mood of imperial accomplishment.

Culture as explanation

My thesis, then, is that culture gradually came to replace nature as an explanatory paradigm for human behavior and organization and indeed for history itself from about the beginning of this century, and that the experiences of and in the Pacific islands played a significant part of this process. The specific ways in which both earlier natural and then cultural explanations in turn have helped form our understanding of Pacific societies and histories will be discussed in the next chapter.

Here I want to consider briefly some implications of the twentieth-century world of cultural explanation—namely, that human-centered disciplines such as history, anthropology, sociology, and their mutated offsprings such as cultural studies, gender studies, consciousness studies have become increasingly trapped in a closed, reflexive loop of explanation. This is reinforced through today's fashionable critical theory and postmodernist analysis generally, which privileges language and discourse in constructing and understanding ourselves, what we are and what we have been. Culture, it seems, and indeed history, is often regarded as little more than a text, a discourse whose full meaning can be grasped only through semiotics and language theory. As a consequence, culture and history have been moved outside or elevated above any hint of naturalist explanation, which is now regarded with deep suspicion as being dangerously essentialist, with ready potential for committing today's heresies of sexism and racism. The fear is that older, reprehensible notions of racial and sexual differences might reassert themselves. But perhaps the baby has been thrown out with the bath water. Culture, as a concept, all too often assumes a discreteness, an exclusiveness, an assumed self-evident, self-sufficient mode of explanation. In practice, the word "culture" has often become merely a descriptive term for itself, used as a slogan or incantation, rather than explanation. And where the rejection of the nineteenth-century naturalist explanation was to avoid perceived racial and other differences among people, cultural explanation now deliberately and fashionably highlights difference. There has, perhaps, been an ironic interchangeability, at least at the semantic level, of the words "culture" and "nature," as colonial times have become postcolonial.

But are there not other ways to describe and interpret culture? Historians and other commentators on culture seldom consider recent findings in some of the brain sciences, such as those examining the role of emotion, or instinct, or genetics in explaining human development, historical events, and social organization and behavior. But such studies draw attention to basic human biological and emotional/psychological similarities rather than differences. And, after all, the term "humanities" is applied to subjects such as history and sociology and anthropology, which presumably assume a common humanity —which is not the same as saying that all humans are the same. We need to consider "modes of thinking," rather than "modes of thought."[62] Culture, writes Henry Plotkin, "is the most complex thing on earth. It has its origins in, and ultimately we will understand it by way of, genetics, development, neurosciences and cognitive science, ecology, ethology and anthropology. We will, though, surely succeed in understanding it one day, because culture is a very natural phenomenon."[63] The utter rejection of naturalist influences on human behavior has been a dominant practice for most of the twentieth century. But more recent findings of evolutionary biology suggest that human behavior and adaptations must also operate within an evolutionary framework.[64] Although it is fashionable to decry nineteenth-century attempts to do so, we perhaps need to make a distinction between their now unacceptable assumptions and findings and their goals of accounting for human activity at least in part within a broad biological and geophysical context.

Emphasis on cultural rather than natural explanation has also logically led to the concept and importance of self that looms so large in twentieth-century life, with all its unprecedented attendant implications for ideas of personal space, rights, and demands. These notions reach extremes, for example, with midcentury existentialism arguing that individuals are "condemned to be free" and need to create themselves. In recent times, New Right ideologues argue that society does not exist, only individuals who should be "privileged to have choice" to enhance their "individual benefit." There is no public good, only private good. Most of us probably believe, more moderately, that individuals, as well as societies, nationalities, cultures, can potentially control and should be enabled to control their own collective identities and destinies. Indeed, in the postcolonial world there are various attempts at redemption for past actions that have destroyed the capacity for self-determination, especially among colonized peoples.

The current culture-centric world also entrenches the idea that we have conquered former difficulties of space and place everywhere on the globe. As a consequence, most modern Western political and economic debate tends to be much more concerned with how, individually and collectively, we might relate to each other, rather than with questions about our place in nature. Yet we also know that beneath the imperatives of global capitalism, our relationship with nature is fraught. It is not a simple environmental issue of whether the remaining "wilderness" can survive. As the deep ecologists have warned us, so far in vain, the issue is really "whether Homo sapiens has a future without wild nature."[65] However we may construct ourselves as cultural beings, we are also just another species, one that is rapidly destroying the planet that has nurtured it.[66] Perhaps some of the nineteenth century's fears about the influences of something called nature were not entirely misplaced. The irony is, perhaps, that if, for example, human-induced global warming is a reality, among the first people to suffer will be those Pacific islanders whose low-lying nation-states will simply disappear beneath the sea. Yet again will Oceania be regarded as a key testing ground for human destiny.

Chapter 3

History as Culture

THE PREVIOUS CHAPTERS have considered how notions of both nature and culture, with reference to Oceania, have variously been constructed and reconstructed in Western discourse. Throughout these processes I have emphasized the complex relationship between theory/expectation and observation/experience. I have suggested that, more often than not, theory/expectation tends to carry far more weight than observation/experience, though there seem to be critical moments when observation and experience can question and modify broad explanatory paradigms. In particular I argued that the changing relative priorities given to nature and culture as explanatory paradigms have, over the past two hundred years, fundamentally altered aspects of the way Western society views and explains the world, and specifically the peoples and places of Oceania. This general point can be illustrated further by examining how Westerners have constructed the history of Oceania and the extent to which such history, like the concepts of nature and culture, similarly reflects Western expectations. Moreover, I will argue that although such expectations may have changed radically over time, the processes and purposes have not. At heart, Pacific history remains something of a morality tale. Today's "knowledge" may be different, but not necessarily superior.

History

This chapter considers history in its technical sense, that is, history generally written by Western, or Western-educated authors for a Western or Western-educated readership. Indeed, history in its conceptual and methodological sense is a product of Western intellectual tradition; it is by no means a universal way of dealing with the past. A distinction is sometimes made between history *of* the Pacific and history *in* the Pacific.[1] This suggests an insider-outsider dichotomy and a tension between hegemonic structure and localized multivocality. I am here concerned with history *of* the Pacific. But history, in this sense, is also now well entrenched within indigenous commentary. There are a very large number of Pacific islands' writers and readers of such history. And, in any case, the distinction between insider and outsider history is now blurred to the point of not being very helpful.

History *of* the Pacific islands is commonly divided into two broad historiographic categories: History that was written in the period up to about the 1950s, often referred to as imperial history, and history that has been written since then, which may be loosely generalized as postimperial or, more commonly, postcolonial history.[2] Historiographic studies tend to emphasize differences between these two categories. But closer examination of their underlying characteristics seems to indicate rather more continuity than change.

Imperial Pacific history

Pacific islands history did not develop a conscious academic identity until the early 1950s. However, the modern discipline has a long-standing pedigree. Historical study of the islands and their indigenous cultures began with descriptions by Western explorers from the fifteenth century and those who followed them in ever-increasing numbers, especially from the early nineteenth century—missionaries, traders, travelers, ethnographers, colonial officials. By the early years of the twentieth century, the scholarly literature outlining the history of the Pacific islands was huge. In hindsight it can be called imperial history because the islands, as geographical, cultural, and historical locations, were defined and examined through imperial eyes.

CULTURAL MAPPING

The subject "region" itself, the islands as a collective entity, only came into being through an imperial perspective that located it on a map of the world. The term "cultural mapping" or "social mapping" is now commonly used to describe this process of describing, naming, categorizing, explaining. It is a process once assumed to be neutral and value-free. It is now seen as a form of cultural violence by the powerful over the powerless. The indigenous inhabitants had no conception of belonging to any "Pacific" entity. The term "Pacific," as a geographic and subject delineater, is a Western construct.[3] And it is still far from being a fixed concept. In Australia and New Zealand, for example, the term "Pacific" generally refers to the Pacific islands. But there is no agreed boundary for these islands, especially in western regions. In practice, they are often deemed to include the eastern half of New Guinea, but they commonly exclude the Indonesian half of New Guinea and the islands of the Southeast Asian archipelago and, invariably, Australia.[4] In North America, the term "Pacific" is more likely not to refer to any islands at all, but to the large countries bordering the Pacific Ocean—the Americas, Russia, Korea, Japan, China.

The long-held subdivisions within the "Pacific islands" are similarly Western constructs. The terms "Micronesia," "Melanesia," and "Polynesia," which had come into currency by the mid-nineteenth century and which have subsequently become deeply imbued with all manner of cultural and racial properties, initially existed only in Western minds. The naming of individual islands, such as New Britain, New Ireland, Savage Island, Admiralty Islands, Easter Island, Sandwich Islands, Cook Islands, was deeply imbued with imperial perceptions and values.[5] And when the Western powers at the end of the nineteenth century carved up the islands into their respective empires, the political boundary lines drawn on their maps often reflected imperial global political maneuvering and cartographic convenience rather than any indigenous entities, identities, and aspirations. As a consequence, many modern, independent Pacific nation-states have geographic boundaries originally created for Western purposes.

Also, Westerners, as fundamentally continental creatures, see islands as tiny dots of land and ignore the surrounding seas. Islands can thus seem small, and therefore insignificant and powerless. Island cultures consequently seem of little consequence. But the surrounding seas, says Epeli Hauʻofa, with their resources and mythological associations, were a part of an islander's consciousness of "territory."[6] The point becomes clearer when modern two hundred–mile economic zones are taken into account, making many island nation-states far bigger than, and, with underseas minerals, perhaps potentially as wealthy as, many of the countries of Europe. Size and significance are often in the eye of the beholder. Concepts of isolation, invariably used in descriptions of the first human discovery and colonization of the islands, are similarly culturally loaded: isolated from what? The distance is invariably measured from continental centers of assumed "civilization."

Precontact history

The imperial gaze also determined the history of the indigenous island cultures. This was generally divided into pre– and post–European contact. Throughout the nineteenth and well into the twentieth century, historians refined the notion that Pacific islanders once shared a common human ancestry with the peoples of Europe. Initially, eighteenth-century classical scholarship likened aspects of Pacific cultures to those of ancient Greece. Early-nineteenth-century scriptural interpretation had Pacific islanders descending from Shem and as one of the Lost Tribes of Israel that eventually wandered off, degenerating, into the Pacific. By mid- to later nineteenth century, comparative mythology and linguistics located them as ancient members of the Indo-European language family, descendants of early Aryan nations in western Asia. Such history told islanders where they had come from, who they were, and how all aspects of their culture might be interpreted. It gave them a chronology for their existence. It explained their religions and oral traditions, typically as garbled versions of biblical events such as the Creation or the Fall or the Great Flood, or as unconscious remnants or survival of their supposed ancient pastoral existence in western Asia. It also gave them origin and migration myths, many of which have subsequently come into indigenous currency, such as the fabled Kaunitoni migration from Africa that peopled Fiji, or the ancestors of the nineteenth-century Hawaiian kings who voyaged from Arabia, or the Great Fleet that came to New Zealand in 1350, or the idea that Pacific islanders originated from South America, or India. It also informed them of their current condition, generally a very degenerate version of what they had once been. And all this new knowledge was thoroughly institutionalized in journals and books, scholarly societies, museums, encyclopedias, opera, art, and literature.[7]

The origins and cultures of Pacific islanders were not persistently and extensively studied for two hundred years merely out of idle or antiquarian curiosity, or for the sake of the knowledge itself. On the contrary, commentators needed to interpret and define the Pacific Other as an act of intellectual appropriation and colonization. But such definition was also a means of locating, defining, and understanding self, both within the span of human progress and amid strange new cultures and places.[8] To regard precontact Pacific societies as remnants of the ancient peoples of Europe, as living fossils, offered both a window directly back to the very infancy of humanity and a mirror to early self. "The Moral Philosopher... who loves to trace the advances of his species through its gradations from savage to civilised life, draws from voyages and travels, the facts from which he is to deduce his conclusions respecting the social, intellectual and moral progress of Man."[9] Such Enlightenment moralizing continued essentially unchanged through the nineteenth century. As Edward Tylor commented in 1867, the "study of the lower races is capable of furnishing most important knowledge about ourselves, about our own habits, customs, laws, principles, prejudices."[10] Much eighteenth- and nineteenth-century ethnology/anthropology was essentially a journey of self-discovery. It still is, though perhaps less consciously so.

CONTACT HISTORY

The concern with historical accounts of islanders in precontact times was but an entree to what was then deemed the centrality of their existence—the arrival of the West. Islanders' history stops with contact. Pacific history then becomes the story of Western arrival and establishment. Most historical studies of the Pacific islands during European contact were usually concerned with the activities of Westerners as agents of empire, expanding Western commercial, religious, and administrative interests into the Pacific and in subsequent international rivalries and colonial rule. The islanders and their cultures, in this triumphal story, were generally relegated to the background. They became objects of Western initiatives, not subjects in their own right. If they were depicted at all it was in a range of crude stereotypes that reflected Western assumptions rather than any indigenous actuality—from noble savages, to ignoble savages, to dying and Romantic savages. Culture contact was often represented as a conflict between active, superior Westerners and passive, inferior islanders. Yet as an ironic undercurrent to the assumption of Western moral and technological superiority there was the persistent notion that Westerners had blundered into a paradise and had destroyed island societies. The notion of a fatal impact and of paradise lost became unquestioned axioms in Pacific studies. Islanders might have been considered degenerate, weak, helpless, flawed by nature and history, but they were not totally without value. In the scale of humankind they were allotted positions of relative superiority and capability over indigenous peoples elsewhere and were indeed ranked relatively close to Caucasians themselves.

This belief in the relative superiority of Pacific islanders in general and Polynesians in particular served to heighten the poignancy of their inability to survive the coming of the West. In turn such concerns led to the powerful stream of paternalism that underpins the predominant theme of the fatal impact in both past and present historical scholarship. Revealed is an ironic ambivalence about Western presence and influence in the islands, even by those most committed to it.

DEPOPULATION—AGAIN

The central event in the imperial history of island societies from the time of Western contact was their depopulation to the presumed point of extinction. Chapter 2 described how the idea that Pacific societies were heading for extinction began in the later eighteenth century and lasted until the 1930s. For most of this very long time, the proposition was taken for granted. I argued that this acceptance resulted less from any quantifiable observation and more from expectations that derived from the discourse about the influence of nature and related assumptions about racial geography and evolutionary theory. Put simply, nature had rendered islanders morally and biologically flawed. They were considered either doomed before Europeans arrived or doomed by that arrival.

It is relatively easy to understand why depopulation theories were in currency. It is much more difficult to explain why the idea fell out of fashion, fairly suddenly in the 1930s. At a superficial level, the reason seems obvious. By the 1930s, colonial governments suddenly realized that many indigenous populations were increasing. The explanation of the time was that Pacific societies had somehow been saved from their long-expected fate by colonial paternalism—the insistence on better sanitation, cleaner water supplies, medical treatment, education, and so on.[11] Such a belief brought a sense of imperial accomplishment, an obligation to humanity duly fulfilled. Yet when one goes and looks for data to support this belief, serious questions arise—namely, saved from what, and how, and by whom or what? These are not easy questions to answer.

To put them into context, there needs to be some consideration of what might or might not have been happening to island populations. First, a distinction needs to be made between past and present definitions of depopulation. In the nineteenth century and the early twentieth, depopulation was understood as an expected and unstoppable decline in population to extinction. In this sense the term "extinctionism" is probably a more appropriate one than "depopulation." Modern demographers have indicated how difficult it actually is for any human population to become extinct, given the dynamics of long-term human reproductive capacity. This capacity can be largely unaffected by reductions in the total size of a population at any particular time. Unless a disease, for example, is persistently age-selective over very many years—and most are not—human populations will generally increase quite quickly over time,[12] unless the increase is consciously prevented by those populations or there are resource limitations or both.

For us today, the term "depopulation" is more appropriate if it is defined as a reduction in population numbers. Generally this is caused by disease. All human societies have experienced it. Europe's population, for example, was probably halved in the fourteenth century. There is no question that periodic reductions in Pacific populations were common, but not universal. Reductions happened both before and after first contact. Contrary to idealized views of life in the pre-European Pacific, certain diseases were endemic in island communities.[13] Certainly many island populations had no initial immunity to introduced epidemic diseases. But how is all this to be quantified? Part of the problem is that there is sometimes little knowledge about the size of island populations at the time of first contact—or rather, that any estimates can be debated. As a generalization, demographic studies have tended to argue against the older, simplistic ideas of catastrophic and universal declines in island populations as a result of the coming of the West. There is better appreciation of complexity relating to location, environment, cultural practice, the timing and nature of Western contact, the epidemiology of diseases, and natural immunology. Some populations did experience significant numerical decline, some remained relatively unaffected, a few increased in size.[14] But the issue of depopulation remains controversial, notably in Hawai'i. Those who support indigenous sovereignty aspirations there and wish to highlight the "horror" of massive population decline after Western contact argue for a huge base population of up to 800,000, as opposed to the more orthodox estimate of 250,000–300,000.[15]

There is a widespread belief that in the early twentieth century indigenous populations in the Pacific experienced a demographic "recovery"—but from what? And if so, why? If it did happen, is it attributable to natural population dynamics combined with growing immunity to the introduced diseases? This seems most likely. Or to changing patterns of disease? This is also possible. Or to better sanitation, cleaner water, or medicine as a result of colonial rule as was claimed at the time? Growing evidence indicates that these claimed improved services, certainly in pre-antibiotic days, were not widely implemented or were relatively ineffective and probably had little overall demographic effect.[16] Tropical medicine in the colonial era was not just a neutral technological activity; its origins, institutional development, and especially its claimed successes were part of the broader ideology of the triumph of colonization in distant, dangerous places.

But debates about depopulation will continue, given both the complexity of the issues and the various current ideological perspectives. My concern here is to focus on the underlying *idea* of extinctionism in the Pacific and to argue for its necessity and inevitability in Western minds.

The fairly sudden end to the belief in extinctionism, in the 1930s, can be explained not just because it seemed that indigenous Pacific populations were not dying out, but more fundamentally because relative priorities given to nature and culture as explanatory categories had altered, with culture coming to ascendency. As argued previously, the Pacific was now a safe place for Westerners: it was both naturally safe and culturally safe. There was the comforting, triumphant, and generally optimistic context of effective colonial control. The extinction argument was ultimately a projection of nineteenth-century Western fears onto the supposedly vulnerable island populations. When these fears disappeared, in the early twentieth century, so too did the sense of the biological vulnerability of Pacific races. In short, extinctionism had a life of its own in educated Western minds. The rise and fall of the *idea* of extinction has its own internal logic and can be examined quite independently of what might or might not have been happening to Pacific islands populations.

Extinctionism was inevitable—at least in Western minds. It was at once a process of both history and nature. It was necessary to fulfill a law of nature and the historical process of realizing the destiny of Western nations in the Pacific. Once those natural and historical purposes had been completed, as they seemed to be in the 1930s, extinctionism ceased to be an issue. It was no longer required. But a basic Western paternal moralizing continued: if island populations had not eventually suffered natural or biological death, there was certainly cultural death. Such arguments were sometimes taken to circular extremes. J. C. Furnas' *Anatomy of Paradise* (1946) wallowed in an insoluble moral dilemma over the "new" problem for islanders of alleged overpopulation: "It looks distressingly as if western medicine and western notions of the sacredness of human life might prove the most destructive of all the things the white men brought."[17]

The fundamental purpose of imperial history was to account for and legitimize colonial dominance. It did so by anticipating and then describing the demise of island populations. It proclaimed the paternal responsibilities and destinies of those Western cultures filling the void and taking over as the new peoples of the Pacific. Imperial history of the Pacific was an empowerment of Western roles and expectations and a disempowerment of the islanders, leaving them either as all-but-extinct peoples or as subservient survivors and grateful supplicants within the beneficent colonial system.

Postcolonial Pacific history

As colonial empires throughout the world collapsed after World War II, historians began to decolonize history. Indigenous peoples were now deemed worthy subjects of serious historical research. In the Pacific, the imperial agenda was abandoned and replaced with an "island-centered" perspective. This new historical agenda was initially fostered at the Australian National University from the 1950s when the Department of Pacific History was established by J. W. Davidson. Instead of studying colonial agents in their imperial context, researchers were to examine island events in an indigenous cultural context.[18] Pacific history henceforth became a study of culture contact and of the consequences of contact for indigenous peoples of Oceania. Within this overall agenda, the emphases and focuses have shifted significantly over the past thirty or so years.[19] For example, in more recent times, the long-standing island-centered perspectives[20] have been modified by awareness of globilization processes, particularly investment, trade, and defense, that have put the islands back into more peripheral situations. The similarly long-standing emphasis on studying precolonial social history has shifted more to considerations of twentieth-century colonial and postindependence political history. Contemporary island situations and conditions have more influence in shaping the priorities and concerns of Pacific historians.[21]

And the fashions and jargon of postmodernism have recently made themselves felt. However, many claims for postmodernism in recent Pacific history are far from novel, leaving its language aside. After all, postcolonial Pacific history is itself a child of thinking about the nature of the Other and postcolonial developments generally. Pacific history since the 1950s and

1960s has been relatively nonauthoritarian, relatively relative, consciously inclusive, aware of pluralities, and certainly deeply reflexive. The alleged sins of modernist history—its singleness, stability, exclusiveness, determinacy—have not been so obvious as perhaps in some other fields of history. Indeed, such characteristics have been positively identified and criticized. Pacific historians for more than a generation have had an introspective self-consciousness and a concern with the cultural/political context of "knowledge," reflected in the considerable literature on Pacific historiography generated by its practitioners. It is also worth noting that what Said did with *Orientalism* in 1979, Bernard Smith had done for Pacific scholarship in 1960 with his *European Vision and the South Pacific*.

But the "harder" dimensions of postmodernism are more problematic for Pacific history, and so far they have not been too influential. The reason is that harder postmodernism rejects any value or moral positioning, and this position does not sit easily with the persistent paternalism of Pacific history and with its associated themes of paradise found or lost. Far more influential in shaping recent Pacific history has been postcolonialism, which is a dimension of postmodernism discourse analysis, but one that also contrasts with postmodernism at certain key points. Some postmodernists argue that Pacific history can no longer be about what happened, or even why it happened, and should be confined to issues of historical re-representation. Postcolonialism, to the contrary, requires a "why and what happened?" metanarrative—in this case, the story of the rise and fall of colonial empires. It thus permits "meanings" over time and place and, implicitly, permits notions of continuities, as opposed to postmodernism's discontinuities. It even permits concepts of "progress" and "improvements," which postmodernism would reject in that values and moralities are deemed relative. Postcolonialism does have a strong sense of "right" and "wrong." There are consciously constructed binary opposites—Western/indigenous, modern/traditional, male/female, colonial/postcolonial. These respective categories are contained within a commonly expressed set of values in academia and beyond, proclaiming that (male) colonialism was wrong. Postcolonial history has the capacity to be politically active and subversive, again in contrast to hard postmodernism's apolitical acceptance of a status quo.

For some time it has been fashionable to deconstruct colonialism's cultures,[22] but not so common to deconstruct postcolonialism's cultures, partly because the enemy is deemed to be elsewhere and partly because postcolonial Pacific history is now so vast and multidisciplinary. However, within this scholarly diversity, it is possible to detect some underlying characteristics. Many of these relate to two areas: the perceived nature of Pacific island societies and causal explanations about processes of culture contact and modernization. Although the particularities may be different from those of imperial history, they still tend to serve the purposes and expectations of those studying Oceania.

Societies

For reasons that were thought perfectly appropriate and correct at the time, imperial Pacific history depicted indigenous societies as fundamentally weak, flawed, and degenerate. In postcolonial history, indigenous societies are more likely to be strong, resilient, adaptable, and vibrant. The underlying reason for the contrast is the fundamental shift in explanatory paradigm from nature to culture and the associated reevaluation of the relative merits of Western and non-Western cultures. The result is that imperial values have been inverted. Today's Pacific historians operate in an ideological environment that tends to privilege the *idea* of indigenous societies. Notions of indigenous culture and custom have been reified.

Chapter 1 argued the case for a twentieth-century reconceptualizing of Pacific nature in the form of the ideal tropical island. Something similar has happened to the idea of Pacific culture.

Both the generality and the specificity of indigenous Pacific culture have commonly been re-ennobled. At its extreme level, perhaps more in the realms of journalism and political rhetoric than academic history, is the claim that Pacific islanders, and indigenous peoples elsewhere, *have* culture, whereas many Westerners, especially in "newer" countries such as Australia and New Zealand, do not. More commonly, islanders are attributed characteristics commonly thought to be lacking in Western society. They are spiritual rather than materialistic; holistic rather than analytical; sharing, caring, communal, and inherently democratic rather than individualistic and self-interested. They are deemed to embody pre-industrial ideals such as honesty and self-sufficiency, as opposed to corrupting values of urban modernity, and they have a closer affinity with nature. There exists a late-twentieth-century version of the noble savage.

Of course such idealizing and privileging of indigenous societies have been recurrent themes in Western thought over the past thousand or more years.[23] The current postcolonial version is a natural and necessary reaction to now outmoded imperial views and colonial practices. Just as imperial history attempted to disempower islanders, postcolonial history is an attempt to reverse that process. It positively supports attempts to improve identity and life for peoples who have been colonized and marginalized. But it does create an environment in which historians sometimes have difficulty depicting multidimensional aspects of indigenous culture in colonial/postcolonial encounter. Criticism or what might be construed as negative comment about island societies tends to be avoided. The idea that island societies, like societies everywhere, may be riven with internal conflicts and contradictions and engage in reprehensible practices is not commonly expressed, by either insiders or outsiders. If such critical comment is made, it is more often than not explained as a consequence of colonialism. There are (at least) three areas where this moral dimension in postcolonial Pacific history can be illustrated.

DEMOCRACY AND "TRADITION"

When the new Pacific island nation-states gained their constitutional independence, mainly in the 1970s and 1980s, there was a heady optimism. Independence had come peacefully and cooperatively. There had been no revolutions, no bloody wars of national liberation. Independence was given, sometimes virtually imposed, rather than taken. Power shifted readily from colonial administrators to existing indigenous political elites. The independence constitutions of the new nation-states were largely informed by Western democratic institutions and values.

But in more recent times, the optimism has diminished. Along with growing economic problems for most Pacific nation-states, there are now very considerable tensions between notions of Western liberal constitutional democracy and some indigenous political values and traditions. The Fiji coups of 1987 were a major wake-up call for historians and others who still viewed the Pacific islands as pleasant, romantic, peaceful locations. These coups, in the name of protecting the rights of indigenous Fijians, caused great consternation to those commentators deeply committed to the commonly held dual ideals of democracy and indigenous rights. In this case, they could not hold both at once.

While the Fiji coups were rather extreme examples in the Pacific context, the underlying tensions between constructs of indigenous "tradition" and "the West," and the politics of Pacific culture, are lively and serious issues in modern scholarship.[24]

"Tradition" is constantly reinvented in all human societies. In Oceania, indigenous tradition has long been constructed by Westerners. It is also constructed from within island societies, often as a necessary anticolonial response and as a basis for an assertion of identity. This identity tends to be expressed more in cultural terms—a cultural nationalism—since political nationalism is often a problematic concept in islands where nation-state boundaries have been arbitrarily imposed, where even concepts of a political nation might have no indigenous precedents, and where so many citizens live outside their state.

Sometimes this process of asserting cultural identity is also used for particular internal purposes that might be regarded as less than noble, such as by some current political elites to maintain their own positions in the face of growing demands by some of their citizens for a more democratic sharing of influence and resources. Traditional indigenous values of status and even "class"—for example, differences between "commoners" and "nobles"—are not always compatible with notions of democracy.

Historians dealing with these matters often feel the need to tread very warily and not give offense. Criticism can so readily lead to accusations of racism.[25] For historians there is the temptation to suspend the critical facility and to appeal to cultural relativism, a situation ethics based on notions of what is loosely referred to as "the Pacific way." Thus, for example, certain practices involving matters of ethnicity, class, or gender or of social, government, and business policy that would be condemned elsewhere in the world are sometimes quietly condoned. As an example, the near-absolute monarchy in Tonga seldom receives the condemnation from crusading democrats that such monarchy might receive if it were elsewhere in the world. In the case of Tonga, it is more likely to be regarded as a "quaint" and beneficent system. Meanwhile, the reification of indigenous tradition, by both insiders and outsiders, has contributed to postcolonial stereotyping. As Stephanie Lawson comments:

> The construction of the dichotomy between "traditional" and "Western" that has been so roundly condemned in anticolonial literature has now been inverted in a form which pervades the rhetoric of those who denounced it in the first place. This unquestioningly produces the same false essentialism which has seduced past generations of scholars into believing that there are determinate characteristics of Western and non-Western "minds."[26]

And the dichotomy is so obviously simplistic anyway. Some of the most "Western" of notions have become thoroughly entrenched within and often central to "tradition," most obviously Christianity. A fundamental problem with academic discussions about Pacific cultural politics is that moral judgments can too readily belie the enormous complexity of issues. The idea of authorative history is no longer acceptable, yet to offer the opposite, the idea of history as an infinitely relative "multivocality,"[27] may in the long run be equally unhelpful. Both strategies are just as inclined to create cardboard cut-outs of their respective selves and others.

ENVIRONMENTALISM

The indigenous Other has periodically been attributed with the inherent capacity to live in total harmony with the (paradisical) environment. This sentiment has been particularly common since the beginnings of the industrial revolution. The recent argument that the industrial economy reinterpreted nature as masculine[28] coincides with the postcolonial romanticizing of indigenous culture in nature and a transference of present-day ecological concerns onto the indigenous Other. There is a common, essentialist notion of indigenous peoples as part of the construct of a redemptive, feminine, nurturing nature. Thus "traditional" Pacific island societies, and particularly Pacific women, are commonly regarded as inherently environmentalist, as living in harmony and equilibrium with their natural world—an object lesson for people today.[29] This view is often advanced more for purposes of a judgment upon the sins of global industrial capitalism than with a concern to understand the dynamics of island societies and their ecosystems. It remains problematic the extent to which arguments about the possibilities of future "sustainable development" in the Pacific and elsewhere can have as an ethos some imagined "traditional Pacific wisdom."[30] The question is less about the "wisdom," more about the concept of "sustainable development."

All human societies over the last ten thousand or more

years have modified and degraded their environments, mainly through tree felling and depletion of fauna.[31] The extent to which this has happened depends on a complex relationship of length of settlement, population numbers, land area and resources, and cultural practice. Pacific societies in pre-European times have not been any different from any others in their varying environmental impacts, ranging from extreme damage on Easter Island to more moderate but still substantial effects on larger forested landscapes in New Zealand or Melanesia. This is not to say that various island communities did not have conservationist practices at a local level and were not highly knowledgeable about their natural environment. It is certainly not an argument against indigenous intellectual property. Nor is it to deny the power of aesthetic appreciation of physical surroundings and sense of holistic belonging, spirituality, and responsibility to nature. But it is to argue that any such attributes and characteristics are not unique to island communities. Where islands were small, and especially on atolls, there were often highly sophisticated conservationist practices and distributive mechanisms. But these need to be assessed in functional terms of the localized mechanics of small-scale human survival and organization rather than in terms that imply that such societies adopted this way of life as if it were some sort of moral choice between an aggressive capitalism and systems of protection and resource distribution. Nor should issues of internal conflict over resources be ignored. Island economics might also involve significant politico-military dynamics. As a consequence, change, whether evolutionary or revolutionary, might be more significant than some older anthropological modeling, with its implications of socioeconomic stability and harmony, might suggest. If anything gave relative protection to many island environments before Western contact, it was their small human populations, in contrast to the mass populations in Europe, or Africa, or Asia.

The arrival of colonial economic systems greatly intensified human impact on the landscape through deforestation associated with pastoralism, plantation economies, mining, and the depletion of species on shore and at sea. The coming of Western commerce did now offer choices, opportunities, and serious challenges to indigenous communities. As elsewhere, the responses to and consequences of the processes of modernization throughout the nineteenth and twentieth centuries are far too complex to reduce to simplistic, moralistic juxtapositioning of an aggressive, industrial, masculinized West overwhelming an opposing, innocent, "natural," feminized Other. From the beginning, the process has thoroughly entangled both outsiders and insiders. In most Pacific societies, and for myriad reasons, there was generally an enthusiastic participation in new commercial activity, whether sandalwood gathering or involvement in the infrastructure of nuclear testing. To lament the processes of modernization for Pacific islanders, a common enough sentiment in tourist brochures as well as more popular history, is to continue to echo aspects of Enlightenment paternalism that would wish somehow to isolate the islands from the rest of humanity.

And postcolonial economic and political realities—whereby the wealth and power of international capital join together with the needs of impoverished island governments—ensure that resource depletion and pollution for short-term gain are just as problematic for Pacific societies now as in the past. The islands still bear what has been termed the "burden of Terra Australis"—the centuries-old notion that the Pacific region existed to be exploited.[32] The recent depletion of Oceania's fish stocks and nuclear testing and dumping come at the end of a long sequence of resource exploitation that began in the late eighteenth century with sea otters and whales. But the overall processes are, again, not unique to the Pacific islands. As Richard Grove notes:

> In the post-colonial period, many "independent" governments, most of them actually run by isolated social elites, have tended to repeat, sometimes even more crudely and brutally, the arrogant environmental mistakes made by their colonial predecessors. Frequently they have displayed the

same disdain and disrespect for indigenous and traditional knowledge. Large-scale prestige projects for dam-building, irrigation, land development and afforestation or deforestation have proved to be just as seductive to post-colonial as to colonial governments, and past mistakes have simply been re-run on much larger scales.[33]

Gender studies

Gender studies, or more specifically studies of women in the Pacific, as in postcolonial history more generally,[34] seek to illustrate the gendered nature of human organization and processes of cultural interaction.[35] As with most other historical investigations, the endeavor reflects a range of current concerns and values that are also projected onto the Other and over time. Thus, for example, gender studies have clearly shown that male sexism is a fundamental ingredient of Enlightenment imperialism and of later colonial systems. The Cook voyages have been a particularly rich source for investigating cultural notions of sexuality and the creation by Western males of Pacific bodies.[36] There have been studies of the role of Pacific women in the wider scheme of Enlightenment theorizing about the nature and processes of civilization and the place of women as either elevating or corrupting influences.[37] There is considerable study of white women and colonial rule, such as that relating to an argument about whether the belated presence of Western women in the Pacific brought about worsening race relations. And there are arguments about the presence of white women being the cause or excuse for drastic, punitive administrative controls over colonized peoples.[38] There is also, as mentioned, the claim that Pacific island women have particular environmental nurturing sensitivities. In general, the modern feminist agenda has been well served with Pacific examples, including recent nuclear testing, the bikini, and the phallic symbolism of nuclear toys.[39] It has also in some circumstances argued for a more active and influential role of women in pre- and early-contact indigenous society. These roles, it is suggested, have been downgraded by

Western male colonizing values and practices, such as the evangelical missionaries' view of women as obedient servants and possessions within the dominant patriarchy, and, it is argued, have consciously been perpetrated by Pacific island males through to the present.[40] The now-unacceptable sexism and domestic oppression in some Pacific societies are thus sometimes explained as a consequence of (male) colonialism.

Causation

In imperial history, islanders in the contact situation were commonly regarded as inferior, weak, passive, helpless, and generally at the mercy of Western agents and influences. The reasons, as I have argued, largely derive from naturalist explanations. By contrast, postcolonial history emphasizes islanders less as victims and more as survivors, resilient and resistant, often determiners of their own fates. The notion of islander agency has been popular for some time now. Consequently, the blanket notions of the fatal impact are now commonly rejected. Islanders are more likely to be seen as adaptive survivors. Again the two notable exceptions tend to be in Hawaiian and New Zealand history. In contrast to most other Pacific islands, both Hawai'i and New Zealand experienced overwhelming Western settlement. Consequently, both the past and present are hotly contested, and "victim" interpretations remain far more common.

The importance of culture as the explanatory paradigm is also critical here. To pick up from the previous chapter, twentieth-century anthropological theory helps to illustrate and validate cultural explanations for social change and human motivation. The centrality of culture has been reinforced with the slipping of an earlier, simplistic functionalism of the 1920s and 1930s into later, more sophisticated forms and eventually to structuralism. Unlike early functionalism, which essentially posited a static and fragile model of precontact indigenous soci-

eties, later functionalism and early structuralism offered a much
more dynamic interpretation of indigenous cultures. Social
change as a result of European contact was less lamented as
studied for its own sake. Further, it was accepted that change
could come as much from within indigenous societies as be
imposed from without. The capacity for resilience and creative
change was emphasized in the Pacific studies of the later Margaret Mead, Ian Hogbin, and C. S. Belshaw.[41] This so-called
acculturation theory led easily to more recent, fashionable
notions of agency, and an emphasis on resistance. These ideas
are often consciously underpinned by reference to counterhege-
monic theory and subaltern studies out of Indian history.[42] Such
ideas are reinforced through a Western postcolonial optimism
and expectation with its perceived liberation of the once-colo-
nized "Other."

Historians have typically offered a range of fairly pragmatic
or utilitarian explanations for human action and social change,
such as economic, social, political, military, religious, technological, and so on, usually in the context of self-interest—whether
of individuals, societies, countries, or cultures. And all these
sorts of explanations have been offered too in postcolonial
Pacific history. While these all fit broadly within what I would
call cultural rather than naturalist explanatory paradigms, in
more recent times a rather more specific notion of cultural
explanation has developed. It focuses on indigenous culture and
has produced explanations that may not be so commonly
applied to nonindigenous societies. Certainly in recent Pacific
history, there has developed a complex structuralist anthropological discourse that, in essence, considers that Other cultures
may have their own self-contained cultural totality with various
systems of rationality and ritualized symbolism or signs. This is
set in opposition to supposedly Western assumptions about universal, utilitarian causation, declared really to be bourgeois
realism or rationalism. This structuralist analysis has considerable hold in Pacific studies.[43]

A recent challenge to it has become the center of a major academic controversy. It concerns the unlikely topic of the death of Captain Cook. For the past few decades, the dominant interpretation, championed by Marshall Sahlins, has been that because Cook first arrived in Hawai'i during the ritual cycle of the beneficent god Lono he was mythically identified as Lono and treated with great respect. But when Cook was forced to return to Hawai'i to repair his ship not long afterward, he did so during the reign of Ku, the god of war, who ritually sacrificed Lono every year. Thus the Hawaiians, the argument goes, were culturally pre-programed or conditioned to kill Cook/Lono.[44] Gananath Obeyesekere has challenged this view, arguing that the notion that the Hawaiians regarded Cook as a god is of European, not Hawaiian, making. It is, he says, "a myth of conquest, imperialism, and civilisation."[45]

> The myth of Cook as the god Lono is fundamentally based on the Western idea of the redoubtable European who is a god to savage peoples. This was further transformed in European thought in the Evangelical idea of idolatry. The later Hawaiian acceptance of this idea is not proof that it was the Hawaiians' idea in the first place. . . . The divinization of Cook is a structure of the long run in European thought, inasmuch as his chiefly deification is a Hawaiian example of the same phenomenon. I am now suggesting that Sahlins's anthropological narrative of the life and death of Cook is not only a theoretical vindication of structural continuity and conjuncture, as he claims, but it is also a continuation, albeit unwitting, of the European myth of the apotheosis of James Cook. Theoretical thought is often enshrined in nontheoretical traditions.[46]

Obeyesekere instead focuses on Cook's attempts to kidnap a Hawaiian chief and his irrational and threatening behavior when the Hawaiian crowd resisted. But it is not a simple debate about why Cook was killed. There is a much more fundamental issue at stake: how can you "know" about the Other and how can you explain why the Other acts as it does? In this case,

Sahlins would argue that "different cultures . . . [have] different rationalities" and as a structuralist anthropologist he can evaluate the evidence to understand them.[47] Obeyesekere, however, adopts a neo-Weberian view of "practical rationality" and argues that he can explain the Hawaiians' actions because humans are linked to a "common biological nature and to perceptual and cognitive mechanisms that are the products thereof."[48] Different societies may have different systems of thought, but not necessarily of thinking. If an irate Cook tries to kidnap a chief and shoots a Hawaiian, one might expect, argues Obeyesekere, the Hawaiians to retaliate. There is already a large critical literature on the Sahlins/Obeyesekere debate, mostly in support of Sahlins (whereas I have felt more comfortable with Obeyesekere's position).[49] What has not been considered by commentators is the extent to which the debate between practical rationality and different rationalities is also in essence something of a continuation of a much broader argument about nature and culture, an argument that has largely been forgotten over the past few generations.

The possibilities for moving beyond structuralism to a poststructuralist analysis in Pacific history do not seem all that promising. Poststructuralism is problematic in postcolonial discourse, particularly with its notions of deference of meaning, and indeed with the meanings of meaning. Even the quest for causation has lost fashion, in the belief that history is not a linked sequence of causally connected events.

In general terms, the emphasis in recent Pacific history is to see problems/issues as being culturally determined and the Other being differently culturally determined. This is usually done in the name of opposing essentialist explanations and of not wishing to impose notions of Western "common sense" onto the actions of the Other. Yet it seems that new essentialisms are being produced. Where imperial history assumed ideas about innate nature, postcolonial history is based on assumptions about innate culture.

Ownership?

There was no question about who owned imperial history. The ownership of postcolonial history is more confused. Charges of "white academic imperialism" have sometimes been heard, but not often. For the most part, independent Pacific communities do not feel themselves particularly culturally endangered, and certainly not by Pacific historians. A number of island governments and communities have welcomed, encouraged, and even honored "outside" historians. Notable exceptions yet again remain in Hawai'i and New Zealand where, since the mid-1970s, haole and pakeha historians have generally not been welcome in writing of Maori and Hawaiian history unless it is to illuminate grievance or promote sovereignty history. Elsewhere there have generally not been antagonistic relations over matters of historical interpretation. Islanders have always been participants in the writing of postcolonial Pacific history, initially through the Australian National University, then in universities in the Pacific islands and beyond. Perhaps now a third or more of active researchers and publishers in Pacific history might claim "islander" status. But to divide today's Pacific historians into simple islander and non-islander categories is not very helpful. There is now a generation of international scholarship caught up in issues of postcoloniality that has long since crossed geographic and cultural boundaries. Like technology, interpretive strategies such as deconstructionism are available to all. The intellectual power relationships and imbalances in the writing of Pacific history, once clear, are now much less so.

There was a time, a few decades ago, when there was considerable expectation about the "inside story," when those on the "other side of the frontier" would produce a radically different version of Pacific history. There were, and sometimes still are, plaintive pleas, invariably by Westerners, for *the* "islander perspective,"[50] assuming some sort of totalized, independent entity of knowledge and experience. This has not materialized. All knowledge is learned knowledge. The assumption that anyone knows all the wisdom of their world simply because they are "islander" or "indigenous" or that the knowledge of knowledgeable individuals represents any generalized indigenous voice or perspective is a patronizing conceit. Different peoples may have different knowledge and perspectives. And Pacific history is certainly a much more diverse enterprise than it once was. But such differences and diversities cannot readily be compressed into the binary categories of islander and non-islander. Furthermore, the notion that a frontier between insider and outsider can define bodies of knowledge and experience requires rethinking. The concept of "two worlds" in Pacific history is persistent. Romantic metaphors of islands and beaches and of cultural and spatial boundaries to be crossed and recrossed remain very deeply ingrained. Even embedded notions of the Pacific paradise, whether accepted or rejected, are predicated on notions of boundaries.

But boundaries as such exist only in the mind. They may make symmetrical sense in history books, but they cannot be seen or be experienced. From the time of first contact, indeed even before it, there existed many, and changing, worlds, especially in the Pacific with its myriad islands and societies. Boundaries, if they existed, would be so numerously layered and complex as to defy representation. The advent and processes of modernization may not have resulted in what some would claim are the ideals of a human melting pot, but neither have they created, in themselves, the ethnic and cultural essentialist juxtapositioning that is often the stuff of Pacific historical scholarship, past and present. That results from an overlay of culturally or politically chosen positioning and boundary fixing—an ironic new variant of cultural mapping, perhaps?

The issue should not be whose past and who owns it, which assumes a contest across a simplistic frontier, but what is owned?[51] In practice, there is a range of opinion from island historians, as from anyone else, from the very radical to the very conservative. In a structural and perceptual sense, so-called insider history has no generalized uniqueness, but sits easily, in all its variety of information and insight, within the context of postcolonial history, and that in itself must contain all the baggage of the colonial experience. Some have claimed this may amount to an appropriation by and of an educated Pacific Other, a change of authors but not of the message. Maybe. And therein lies the basis for the debate about whether postcolonial history is postcolonial. Most important, I think, is that islanders who want to represent their past in some alternative way simply do so. Expression of identity in island communities continues overwhelmingly to be in oral tradition, song, dance, theater, and, in recent decades, also in an outpouring of plays, poems, short stories, and novels. There is a massive creative literature in English in the Pacific. The conscious writing of history is a minority code. Even the incorporation of such material into history must necessarily change its context. History is a strategy of selecting, prioritizing, and organizing according to a range of Western assumptions about causation and change over time. The idea of a historical representation of multivocality is a contradiction in terms. This is not an argument against multivocality, but an argument that although its narration may be about the past, it is not necessarily history.

Embedded in issues of ownership are assumptions about who Pacific history is *for*. Those teaching Pacific history are inevitably asked how many Pacific islanders are in their classes. No one ever asks how many Russian or U.S. students are in classes in Russian history or U.S. history. Pacific history, it is invariably assumed, must somehow be *for* Pacific islanders. Such a claim was never more clearly articulated than by Harry Maude almost thirty years ago:

> [Pacific history] has a very practical and therapeutic role to enact in assisting the rehabilitation of the Pacific peoples at the end of a traumatic era of European political, economic and technological ascendency by renewing their self-respect and providing them with a secure historical base from which to play their part as responsible citizens of independent or self-governing communities in a new world.[52]

In today's postcolonial world, such sentiments, still commonly heard, can be double-edged, revealing a deep-seated paternalism.

Conclusion

All history is a story. As Hayden White has reminded us, histories, like every other kind of story, have very limited plots, explanations, and ideologies. Pacific history, whether it be imperial or postcolonial, displays a remarkable underlying consistency. To be sure there are major shifts in subjects and methodologies and values and conclusions between imperial and postcolonial history. But at the very heart of all Pacific history, whether imperial or postcolonial, lies a morality tale. It is about the meeting of two perceived entities—the West and Pacific peoples. These entities are personified, variously, into forces of good and evil that engage in a prolonged contest. The metaphorical/allegorical message is underpinned by the more specific tropes of metonymy and synecdoche. Hence Cook, for example, stands for Enlightenment imperialism, just as Enlightenment imperialism is Cook. And the setting remains an exotic paradise, whether lost or found or rejected outright. It seems that the intellectual uses the Pacific islands are put to are not unlike those exemplified by Shakespeare, Swift, Defoe, Melville . . .

Pacific history is fundamentally about the idea of Western civilization, its perceived rise and fall, its fears and triumphs, and its creation of a Pacific Other onto which are projected and tested its various priorities and expectations. Its particular concerns may have changed dramatically over two hundred years, from such issues as civilization, imperial destiny, and race survival to matters like racism, sexism, environmentalism, and political rights, but the process and purpose remain remarkably constant. In particular, postcolonial Pacific history's claims to have crossed to the other side of the frontier remain unconvincing, mainly because the frontier, as both a line in the sand

and as an insider-outsider delineater, is a construct. Nor is post-colonialism's claim for a unique reflexivity justified, since a very conscious reflexivity was also a notable feature of imperial history (though not necessary in ways we would approve of now). And postcolonialism's Other is just as essentialist as that of imperial history, even if that Other is multiple, local, variable. Both imperial and postcolonial Pacific history link what we would now call social policy priorities and concerns to an idea of history itself.

The role of imperial history was to be an agent of imperial policy. The role of postcolonial history is to be an agent of post-coloniality. Where imperial history was preemptive, postcolonial history is redemptive. Both make journeys toward self. The latter is often just as morally certain as the former, though ironically is often less conscious of itself.

If there is a linking ideology between imperial and post-colonial Pacific history, it is paternalism in its many guises. Enlightenment paternalism toward Pacific peoples slipped readily into a nineteenth-century concern for the demise of island populations and a justification for imperial annexation and colonial rule. When extinctionism became irrelevant, and cultural rather than natural explanation came in vogue, paternal angst flourished instead on the idea of the islanders' cultural rather than biological demise. If anything, paternalism as an administrative imperative and as a mode of historical interpretation reached new heights, particularly during and after World War II in the Pacific islands. These sentiments are still expressed in certain quarters.

Postcolonial Pacific history, ostensibly rejecting paternalism, has created its own variants of it. It has done so by deconstructing both colonialism and the writing of imperial history, revealing characteristics that in today's world are not acceptable. In addition, it has created expectations of a monolithic "indigenous" agency and liberation according to its own set of ideals and expectations.

I rest my case for history as culture.

Notes

Chapter 1: Nature as Culture

1. Louis-Antoine de Bougainville, *A Voyage Round the World . . . in the Frigate "La Boudeuse" and the Store Ship "L'Etoile". . . ,* trans. J. R. Forster (London: J. Nourse and T. Davies, 1772), 228–229.

2. Ibid., 257.

3. J. C. Beaglehole, ed., *The "Endeavour" Journal of Joseph Banks 1768–1771* (Sydney: Angus and Robertson, 1963), 1:252, 342.

4. J. C. Beaglehole, ed., *The Voyage of the "Endeavour" 1768–1771* (London: Hakluyt Society, Kraus Reprint, 1988), 1:187.

5. Bernard Smith, *The European Vision and the South Pacific 1768–1850: A Study in the History of Art and Ideas* (London: Oxford University Press, 1960); and *Imagining the Pacific: In the Wake of the Cook Voyages* (New Haven, Conn.: Yale University Press, 1992).

6. Simon Schama, *Landscape and Memory* (London: Harper Collins, 1995), 61. There is a very large literature on the "cultural" reading of landscape/environment. Suggestive works for this chapter include Eric Hirsch and Michael O'Hanlon, eds., *The Anthropology of Landscape: Perspectives on Place and Space* (Oxford: Clarendon Press, 1995); Keith Thomas, *Man and the Natural World: Changing Attitudes in England 1500–1800* (London: Allen Lane, 1983); Raymond Williams, "Ideas of Nature," in *Ecology, the Shaping Enquiry,* ed. Jonathan Benthall (London: Longman, 1972), 146–164; James Duncan and David Ley, eds., *Place/Culture/Representation* (London: Routledge, 1993); Alexander Wilson, *The Culture of Nature: North American Landscape from Disney to Exxon Valdez* (Cambridge, Mass.: Blackwell, 1992); Max Oelschlaeger, *The Idea of Wilderness: From Prehistory to the Age of Ecology* (New Haven, Conn.: Yale University Press, 1991); Roderick Nash, *Wilderness and the American Mind,* rev. ed. (New Haven, Conn.: Yale University

Press, 1973); N. Jardine, J. A. Secord, and E. C. Spary, eds., *Cultures of Natural History* (Cambridge: Cambridge University Press, 1996).

Although this chapter concentrates on the idea of the tropical Pacific island, there are some instructive comparisons to be made with another created cultural space—the polar regions. For an introduction see Francis Spufford, *I May Be Some Time: Ice and the English Imagination* (London: Faber and Faber, 1996). See also Barry Lopez, *Arctic Dreams: Imagination and Desire in a Northern Landscape* (New York: Charles Scribner, 1986).

7. Richard H. Grove, *Green Imperialism: Colonial Expansion, Tropical Island Edens and the Origins of Environmentalism 1600–1860* (Cambridge: Cambridge University Press, 1995). See also Valerie I. J. Flint, *The Imaginative Landscape of Christopher Columbus* (Princeton, N.J.: Princeton University Press, 1992).

8. John Prest, *The Garden of Eden: The Botanic Garden and the Re-creation of Paradise* (New Haven, Conn.: Yale University Press, 1981); and Grove, *Green Imperialism.*

9. Grove, *Green Imperialism,* 23.

10. Flint, *Imaginative Landscape;* and Stephen Greenblatt, *Marvelous Possessions: The Wonder of the New World* (Chicago: University of Chicago Press, 1991).

11. Letter of 1498, quoted in J. M. Cohen, *The Four Voyages of Christopher Columbus* (London: Cresset, 1969).

12. Letter III (1502), in Luciano Formisano, ed., *Letters from a New World: Amerigo Vespucci's Discovery of America* (New York: Marsilio, 1992), 31.

13. Grove, *Green Imperialism.*

14. David Fausett, *Writing the New World: Imaginary Voyages and Utopias of the Great Southern Land* (Syracuse, N.Y.: Syracuse University Press, 1993).

15. Prest, *Garden of Eden,* 27, 29.

16. Cecil Jane, trans., *The Journal of Christopher Columbus* (London: Orion Press, 1960), 40.

17. Ibid., 196.

18. Grove, *Green Imperialism,* 43–44. See also Grove, *Ecology, Climate and Empire* (Cambridge: White Horse Press, 1997), chap. 2.

19. Flint, *Imaginative Landscape.*

20. Stephen Bann, "From Captain Cook to Neil Armstrong: Colonial exploration and the structure of landscape," in *Reading Landscape: Country, City, Capital,* ed. Simon Pugh (Manchester: Manchester University Press, 1990), 214–215.

21. Neil Rennie, *Far-fetched Facts: The Literature of Travel and the Idea of the South Seas* (Oxford: Clarendon Press, 1995).

22. Diana Loxley, *Problematic Shores: The Literature of Islands* (New York: St. Martin's Press, 1990), xi.

23. Ernst Bloch, *The Principle of Hope,* trans. Neville Plaice et al., 3 vols. (Cambridge, Mass.: MIT Press, 1986), 1:24. See also 2:746–794.

As an example, children's readings of *Robinson Crusoe,* usually in adapted form, and whose images frequently last into adulthood, are often couched in an adventurous Romanticism. But a serious reading of the novel will find little that is attractive about the island. There is actually very little description of it. And with the exception of a couple of paragraphs where Crusoe waxes lyrical over a "delicious vale" that "looked like a planted garden" (Daniel Defoe, *Robinson Crusoe* [London: Everyman's Library, 1964], 74), the natural environment is hardly idyllic. On the contrary, Crusoe inhabits a "dismal unfortunate island . . . the Island of Despair" (53). It is a place of "storms and hurricanes of wind" (73) and earthquakes (60). He assumes that it harbors "beasts" and much of his time is spent building fortifications and hiding places. He is "a prisoner, lock'd up with the eternal bars and bolts of the ocean, in an uninhabited wilderness" (84). Crusoe survives and prospers in spite of the island, not because of it. Its resources, such as grapes, turtles, and goats, and its rainfall provide the basic raw materials for his successful colonization but it is his efforts that are critical. Furthermore his material comforts are also very much augmented by tools and supplies he salvaged in great quantities from his wrecked ship. It is a tale of successful human endeavor within and upon the natural environment. Nature is worked upon, improved, exploited by Crusoe; it does not provide for him unassisted. His island is a potentially hostile object rather than benevolent subject.

24. There is a considerable literature on how human growth is rooted in both childhood and wild landscape generally; see Gary Paul Nabhan, *The Geography of Childhood: Why Children Need Wild Places* (Boston: Beacon Press, 1994).

25. William Eisler, *The Furthest Shore: Images of Terra Australis from the Middle Ages to Captain Cook* (Cambridge: Cambridge University Press, 1995).

26. Colin Jack-Hinton, *The Search for the Islands of Solomon 1567–1838* (Oxford: Clarendon Press, 1969); O. H. K. Spate, *The Spanish Lake* (Canberra: Australian National University Press, 1979).

27. Fausett, *Writing the New World;* and Fausett, *Images of the Antipodes in the Eighteenth Century: A Study in Stereotyping* (Amsterdam: Rodopi, 1995).

28. Lord Amherst and Basil Thomson, eds., *The Discovery of the Solomon Islands by Alvaro de Mendana in 1568* (London: Hakluyt Society, 1901).

29. Clements Markham, ed., *The Voyages of Pedro Fernandez de Quiros 1595 to 1604* (London: Hakluyt Society, 1904), 1:478, 479.

30. Eisler, *The Furthest Shore*. See also Glyndwr Williams, "Buccaneers, castaways, and satirists: The South Seas in the English consciousness before 1750" in *The South Pacific in the Eighteenth Century: Narratives and Myths*, ed. Jonathan Lamb, special edition of *Eighteenth Century Life* 18:3 (1994), 114–128; and his *The Great South Sea: English Voyages and Encounters 1570–1750* (New Haven, Conn.: Yale University Press, 1997). However, I do not agree with Williams' view (182–183) that the "Dream of Islands" was essentially an English construct developed in the Pacific. For subsequent "dreaming" of islands see Gavan Daws, *A Dream of Islands: Voyages of Self-discovery in the South Seas* (Milton, Queensland: Jacaranda Press, 1980).

31. There is also an interesting and much later variant of paradise lost, or rather paradise sunk. The nineteenth-century predilection for sunken-continent theories led, for example, to biologist Ernst Haeckel's claim that "Paradise"—the *"single primaeval home* for mankind"—was tropical Lumuria, a now sunken continent in the Indian Ocean; see his *History of Creation, Or the Development of the Earth and Its Inhabitants by the Action of Natural Causes* (London: Kegan Paul, Trench, 1883), 325–326 (emphasis in original). There are also numerous twentieth-century books on the lost continent in the Pacific (Mu, or Lemuria) as the original location of the Biblical paradise, e.g., James Churchward, *The Lost Continent of Mu* (Albuquerque, N.M.: BE Books, [1931], 1991).

32. There is a huge and ongoing deconstructionist literature about such Pacific texts. Two recent examples are Rod Edmond, *Representing the South Pacific: Colonial Discourse from Cook to Gauguin* (Cambridge: Cambridge University Press, 1997); and Vanessa Smith, *Literary Culture and the Pacific: Nineteenth Century Textual Encounters* (Cambridge: Cambridge University Press, 1998).

33. A. Grove Day, *Louis Becke* (New York: Twayne Publishers, 1966); and idem, ed., *Louis Becke: South Sea Supercargo* (Brisbane: Jacaranda Press, n.d.).

34. Day, *Louis Becke*, 36.

35. Louis Becke, "Challis the doubter," in *By Reef and Palm* (Sydney: Angus and Robertson, 1955), 21.

36. Becke, "The revenge of Macy O'Shea," ibid., 44–45.

37. Becke, "The fate of the *Alida*," ibid., 115.

38. Becke, "Brantley of Vahitahi," ibid., 175.

39. Asterisk [Robert James Fletcher], *Isles of Illusion: Letters from the South Seas* (London: Century Hutchinson, 1986), 35, 42, 137, 259.

40. Ibid., 76.

41. Ibid., 108.

42. Robert Louis Stevenson, *In the South Seas* [1896] (London: Hogarth Press, 1987).

43. Bronislaw Malinowski, *A Diary in the Strict Sense of the Term* (London: Routledge and Kegan Paul, 1967), e.g., 69, 155, 161, 162.

44. Ibid., 16.

45. Christina A. Thompson, "Anthropology's Conrad: Malinowski in the tropics and what he read," *Journal of Pacific History* 30:1 (1995), 53–75.

46. John Macmillan Brown, *Peoples and Problems of the Pacific* (London: T. Fisher Unwin, 1927), 1:1, 10.

47. Ibid., 138.

48. Useful sources on tourism are Ngaire Douglas, *They Came for Savages: 100 Years of Tourism in Melanesia* (Lismore, NSW: Southern Cross University Press, 1996); Norman Douglas and Ngaire Douglas, "Tourism in the Pacific: Historical factors," in *Tourism in the Pacific: Issues and Cases,* ed. Michael C. Hall and Stephen J. Page (London: International Thomson Business Press, 1996); Dennison Nash, *Anthropology of Tourism* (Oxford: Pergamon, 1996); Valerie L. Smith, *Hosts and Guests: The Anthropology of Tourism,* 2d ed. (Philadelphia: University of Pennsylvania Press, 1989); Anna Steven, ed., *Pirating the Pacific: Images of Travel, Trade and Tourism* (Sydney: Powerhouse Publishing, 1993); John Urry, *The Tourist Gaze: Leisure and Travel in Contemporary Societies* (London: Sage, 1990).

49. John Wear Burton, *The Fiji of Today* (London: Charles H. Kelly, 1910), 34.

50. Quoted in Eugenie Laracy and Hugh Laracy, "Beatrice Grimshaw: Pride and prejudice in Papua," *Journal of Pacific History* 12:3–4 (1977), 162.

51. W. Lavallin Puxley, *Green Islands in Glittering Seas* (London: George Allen and Unwin, 1925), 18.

52. A Lady Member of the Melanesian Mission, *The Isles That Wait* (London: Society for Promoting Christian Knowledge, 1915), 10.

53. The idea of depopulation will be considered in chaps. 2 and 3.

54. Brown, *Peoples and Problems,* 1:175; 2:242. On Anglo-Saxon destiny in the Pacific see also H. Stonehewer Cooper, *Coral Lands,* vol. 2 (London: R. Bentley, 1882).

55. Paul McGuire, *Westward the Course: The New World of Oceania* (Melbourne: Oxford University Press, 1942), n.p.

56. Gordon Maitland, "The two sides of the camera lens: Nineteenth century photography and the indigenous people of the South Pacific," *Photofile South Pacific,* 1988, 47–60.

57. T. W. Whitson, ed., *The Tourists' Vade Mecum (Illustrated) Being a Handbook to the Services of the Union Steamship Company . . .*

Together with an Index Guide (Dunedin: Union Steam Ship Company of New Zealand, 1912), 123. See also *The Commercial Directory and Tourists' Guide to the South Pacific Islands 1903–4* (Sydney: T. B. Dineen, 1904), 79.

58. Whitson, *Tourists' Vade Mecum,* 124.

59. Ibid., 134.

60. Ibid., 147.

61. Ibid., 137.

62. Winifred Ponder, *An Idler in the Islands* (Sydney: Cornstalk Publishing, 1924), 7.

63. Peter J. Schmitt, *Back to Nature: The Arcadian Myth in Urban America* (New York: Oxford University Press, 1969); G. Altmeyer, "Three ideas of nature in Canada, 1899–1914," *Journal of Canadian Studies* 11:3 (1976), 21–36. See also Gunther Barth, *Fleeting Moments: Nature and Culture in American History* (Oxford: Oxford University Press, 1990).

64. Douglas Booth, "Healthy, economic, disciplined bodies: Surf-bathing and surf lifesaving in Australia and New Zealand, 1890–1950," *New Zealand Journal of History* 32:1 (1998), 43–58.

65. Sean Brawley and Chris Dixon, "'The Hollywood Native': Hollywood's construction of the South Seas and wartime encounters with the South Pacific," *Sites* 27 (1993), 15–29.

66. Andrew Ross, "Cultural preservation in the Polynesia of the Latter-Day Saints," in *The Chicago Gangster Theory of Life: Nature's Debt to Society* (London: Verso, 1994), 21–98.

67. Elizabeth Buck, *Paradise Remade: The Politics of Culture and History in Hawai'i* (Philadelphia: Temple University Press, 1993).

68. See Carolyn Merchant, *The Death of Nature: Women, Ecology, and the Scientific Revolution* (New York: Harper, 1990).

69. Thor Heyerdahl, *Fatu Hiva: Back to Nature* (London: George Allen and Unwin, 1974), 11, 59, 103, 369, 370, 381.

70. Tom Neil, *An Island to Oneself: The Story of Six Years on a Desert Island* (London: Collins, 1966), 19.

71. Paul Theroux, *The Happy Isles of Oceania: Paddling the Pacific* (London: Hamish Hamilton, 1992), 6.

72. TEAL advertising pamphlet, 1950s, Ephemera G 155, Auckland Institute and Museum. See also Nancy Phelan, *Pieces of Heaven: In the South Seas* (St. Lucia: University of Queensland Press, 1996).

73. "Flying Boats," *New Zealand Geographic* 40 (1998), 125.

74. Alastair Shephard, "The Coral Route story: A history of TEAL's flying boat service in the Pacific 1950–1960" (M.A. thesis, Auckland University, 1994), 13.

75. Urry, *Tourist Gaze,* 139–140.

Chapter 2: Culture as Nature

1. Clarence J. Glacken, *Traces on the Rhodian Shore: Nature and Culture in Western Thought from Ancient Times to the End of the Eighteenth Century* (Berkeley: University of California Press, 1967).

2. N. Jardine, J. A. Secord, and E. C. Spary, eds., *Cultures of Natural History* (Cambridge: Cambridge University Press, 1966); see esp. chap. 2.

3. Baron de Montesquieu, *The Spirit of Laws* [1748], trans. Thomas Nugent (New York: Hafner, 1949), 221–224.

4. David Philip Miller and Peter Hanns Reill, eds., *Visions of Empire: Voyages, Botany, and Representations of Nature* (Cambridge: Cambridge University Press, 1996).

5. Johann Reinhold Forster, *Observations Made during a Voyage Round the World* [1778], ed. Nicholas Thomas, Harriet Guest, and Michael Dettelbach (Honolulu: University of Hawai'i Press, 1996); see esp. chap. 6.

6. Ibid., 196 (emphasis in original).

7. Michael Hoare, *The Tactless Philosopher: Johann Reinhold Forster 1729–1798* (Melbourne: Hawthorn Press, 1976), 144, 311; Thomas Bendysche, *The Anthropological Treatises of Johann Friedrich Blumenbach* (Boston: Milford House, 1973), 264–266.

8. Alexander von Humboldt, *Cosmos: A Sketch of the Physical Description of the Universe,* trans. E. C. Otté (London: Henry G. Bohn, 1864), 1:327.

9. Forster, *Observations,* 342.

10. A useful narrative is George Tatham, "Geography in the nineteenth century," in *Geography in the Twentieth Century: A Study of Growth, Fields, Techniques, Aims and Trends,* ed. Griffith Taylor (London: Methuen, 1960), 28–69. See also R. J. Johnston, *Geography and Geographers: Anglo-American Human Geography since 1945,* 2d ed. (Baltimore: Edward Arnold, 1985).

11. Humboldt, *Cosmos,* 1:3.

12. Ibid., 1:334 (emphasis in original). On Humboldt see also Michael Dettelbach, "Global physics and aesthetic empire: Humboldt's physical portrait of the tropics," in *Visions of Empire: Voyages, Botany, and Representations of Nature,* ed. David Philip Miller and Peter Hanns Reill (Cambridge: Cambridge University Press, 1996), 258–292.

13. Henry Thomas Buckle, *Introduction to the History of Civilization in England* (London: George Routledge and Sons, 1904), 87.

14. Ibid.

15. Quoted in Redmond O'Hanlon, *Joseph Conrad and Charles*

Darwin: The Influence of Scientific Thought on Conrad's Fiction (Edinburgh: Salamander Press, 1984), 27.

16. Quoted in Nicholas Thomas, "'On the varieties of the human species': Forster's comparative ethnology," in Forster, *Observations Made during a Voyage Round the World,* xxiii.

17. Translator's preface to J. J. H de Labillardière, *Voyage in Search of La Pérouse, Performed by the Order of the Constituent Assembly during the Years 1791, 1792, 1793, and 1794* (London: Stockdale, 1800), vii.

18. Olive Wright, ed., *New Zealand 1826–1827 from the French of Dumont D'Urville* (Wellington: O. Wright, 1950), 126–127.

19. "Mobs," *Blackwoods,* 1893, quoted in Daniel Pick, *Faces of Degeneration: A European Disorder, c.1848–c.1918* (Cambridge: Cambridge University Press, 1993), 223.

20. Robert A. Nye, "Degeneration and the medical model of culture crisis in the French Belle Epoque," in *Political Symbolism in Modern Europe,* ed. Seymour Drescher et al. (New Brunswick, N.J.: Transaction Books, 1982), 19–41. See also Pick, *Faces of Degeneration.*

21. Philip D. Curtin, "'The White Man's grave': Image and reality, 1750–1850," *Journal of British Studies* 1:1 (1961), 94–110. See also Curtin, *Death by Migration: Europe's Encounter with the Tropical World in the Nineteenth Century* (Cambridge: Cambridge University Press, 1989).

22. David N. Livingstone, "Climate's moral economy: Science, race and place in post-Darwinian British and American Geography," in *Geography and Empire,* ed. Anne Godlewska and Neil Smith (Oxford: Blackwell, 1994), 132–154.

23. Benjamin Kidd, *The Control of the Tropics* (London: Macmillan, 1898), 30.

24. Griffith Taylor, "Racial geography," in *Geography in the Twentieth Century,* ed. Taylor, 433–462a.

25. Ellsworth Huntington, "Climate and the evolution of civilization," in *The Evolution of Earth and Man,* ed. George Alfred Baitsell (New Haven, Conn.: Yale University Press, 1929), 330–383.

26. A. Grenfell Price, *White Settlers in the Tropics* (New York: American Geographical Society, 1939), 199.

27. Ronald L. Meek, *Social Science and the Ignoble Savage* (Cambridge: Cambridge University Press, 1976).

28. Peter J. Bowler, *Darwinism* (New York: Twayne, 1993).

29. Edward B. Tylor, *Primitive Culture: Researches into the Development of Mythology, Philosophy, Religion, Art, and Custom* (London: John Murray, 1871), 1:2, 28.

30. Derek Freeman, *Margaret Mead and Samoa: The Making and Unmaking of an Anthropological Myth* (Canberra: Australian National University Press, 1983), 21.

31. Quoted ibid., 8.

32. K. R. Howe, "The intellectual discovery and exploration of Polynesia," in *From Maps to Metaphors: The Pacific World of George Vancouver,* ed. Robin Fisher and Hugh Johnston (Vancouver: UBC Press, 1993), 245–262; see also Howe, "Some origins and migrations of ideas leading to the Aryan Polynesian theories of Abraham Fornander and Edward Tregear," *Pacific Studies* 11:2 (1988), 67–81.

33. Roy MacLeod and Philip E. Rehbock, eds., *Nature in Its Greatest Extent: Western Science in the Pacific* (Honolulu: University of Hawai'i Press, 1988); and idem, *Evolutionary Theory and the Natural History of the Pacific: Darwin's Laboratory* (Honolulu: University of Hawai'i Press, 1994).

34. David Quammen, *The Song of the Dodo: Island Biogeography in an Age of Extinctions* (New York: Scribner, 1996), 436.

35. K. R. Howe, "The fate of the 'savage' in Pacific historiography," *New Zealand Journal of History* 11:2 (1977), 137–154; and Howe, "The intellectual discovery."

36. Beaglehole, ed., *The Voyage of the "Endeavour,"* 99.

37. George Forster, *A Voyage Round the World* (London: B. White, 1777), 368.

38. Howe, "Fate of the 'savage.'"

39. M. Russell, *Polynesia: A History of the South Seas* (London: T. Nelson, 1853), 469.

40. A. L. A. Forbes, "On the extinction of certain races of men," *New South Wales Medical Gazette* 3 (1873), 321.

41. F. D. Fenton, *Suggestions for a History of the Origins and Migrations of the Maori People* (Auckland: H. Brett, 1885), 122.

42. Percy Smith, *Hawaiki: The Original Home of the Maoris* (Christchurch: Whitcombe and Tombs, 1904), 138.

43. Stevenson, *In the South Seas,* 40–42.

44. For example, R. W. Cilento, "The depopulation of the Pacific," *Proceedings of the Pan-Pacific Science Congress* 2 (1923), 1395–1399; George Henry Lane-Fox Pitt-Rivers, *The Clash of Culture and the Contact of Races* (London: George Routledge and Sons, 1927); W. H. R. Rivers, ed., *Essays on the Depopulation of Melanesia* (Cambridge: Cambridge University Press, 1922).

45. Stephen H. Roberts, *Population Problems of the Pacific* (London: George Routledge, 1927), 60, 63.

46. Brown, *Peoples and Problems of the Pacific,* 1:126–127. See also his *Riddle of the Pacific* (London: T. Fisher Unwin, 1924), 289–301.

47. George Tatham, "Environmentalism and possibilism," in *Geography in the Twentieth Century,* ed. Taylor, 128–162.

48. Henrika Kuklick, "The color blue: From research in the Torres

Strait to an ecology of human behavior," in *Evolutionary Theory and the Natural History of the Pacific: Darwin's Laboratory,* ed. Roy MacLeod and Philip E. Rehbock (Honolulu: University of Hawai'i Press, 1994), 339–367.

49. Quoted ibid., 355.

50. For a less optimistic view of the consequences of this expedition see George W. Stocking, *After Tylor: British Social Anthropology 1888–1951* (Madison: University of Wisconsin Press, 1995), 111–115.

51. Margaret Mead, *Coming of Age in Samoa: A Study of Adolescence and Sex in Primitive Societies* (Harmondsworth: Penguin, 1963).

52. Freeman, *Margaret Mead and Samoa.*

53. Bronislaw Malinowski, *Argonauts of the Western Pacific: An Account of Native Enterprise and Adventure in the Archipelagoes of Melanesian New Guinea* (London: George Routledge, 1932).

54. Kuklick, "The color blue"; Stocking, *After Tylor,* chaps. 6, 7.

55. F. E. Williams, "Creed of a government anthropologist," in *"The Vailala Madness" and Other Essays,* ed. Erik Schwimmer (St. Lucia: University of Queensland Press, 1976), 405. I thank Hank Nelson for this reference.

56. W. H. R. Rivers, "The psychological factor," in *Essays on the Depopulation of Melanesia,* ed. Rivers, 107; see also Malinowski, *Argonauts,* 465.

57. Rivers, "The psychological factor," 94, 107–109.

58. Cooper, *Coral Lands,* 2:299–300.

59. W. J. Durrad, "The depopulation of Melanesia," in *Essays on the Depopulation of Melanesia,* ed. Rivers, 24.

60. T. R. St. Johnston, *The Islands of the Pacific, or the Children of the Sun* (New York: Appleton, 1921), 11–12 (emphasis in original).

61. Stocking, *After Tylor,* 103; see also chap. 8.

62. This phrase comes from Gananath Obeyesekere, *The Apotheosis of Captain Cook: European Mythmaking in the Pacific* (Princeton, N.J.: Princeton University Press, 1992), 21. The broader intellectual implications of Obeyesekere's case study of Cook's death will be discussed in the following chapter.

63. Henry Plotkin, *The Nature of Knowledge: Concerning Adaptations, Instinct and the Evolution of Intelligence* (London: Penguin, 1994), 227. See also Steve Mithen, *The Prehistory of the Mind: A Search for the Origins of Art, Religion and Science* (London: Thames and Hudson, 1996); Peter B. Neubauer and Alexander Neubauer, *Nature's Thumbprint: The New Genetics of Personality* (New York: Addison-Wesley, 1990); Daniel Goleman, *Emotional Intelligence* (London: Bloomsbury, 1996); Steven Pinker, *How the Mind Works* (New York: Norton, 1997).

64. Indeed, it seems likely that some of the more insightful observations about human history will come from nonhistorians. As one recent excellent example, see Jarad Diamond, *Guns, Germs and Steel: A Short History of Everybody for the Last 13,000 Years* (London: Vintage, 1998). See also his *Rise and Fall of the Third Chimpanzee* (London: Radius, 1991).

65. Max Oelschlaeger, *The Idea of Wilderness: From Prehistory to the Age of Ecology* (New Haven, Conn.: Yale University Press, 1991), 327.

66. John Leslie, *The End of the World: The Science and Ethics of Human Extinction* (London: Routledge, 1996); Bill McKibben, *The End of Nature* (London: Viking, 1990)..

Chapter 3: History as Culture

1. Greg Dening, "History *in* the Pacific," *The Contemporary Pacific* 1:1 and 2 (1989), 134–139.

2. The term "postcolonial Pacific history" can be confusing. Whether postcolonial really means postcolonial in the sense that a different and fundamentally indigenous-led value structure is (or can be) adopted remains decidedly an open question. I use the term "postcolonial history" mainly as a label to locate it chronologically in Pacific historiography, that is, in the period since about World War II. To some extent it is a misleading term in that colonial rule for most Pacific islands actually lasted until the 1970s and 1980s. Other terms have been variously applied over the past thirty years, such as "island centered"; the "Canberra school," which refers to the development of the first academic Department of Pacific History, at the Australian National University; and "modern Pacific history." I would personally prefer to use the term "postimperial Pacific history," but this is not in common usage.

3. O. H. K. Spate, "'South Sea' to 'Pacific Ocean': A note on nomenclature," *Journal of Pacific History* 12:4 (1977), 205–211; and Spate, "The Pacific as an artefact," in *The Changing Pacific: Essays in Honour of H. E. Maude*, ed. Niel Gunson (Melbourne: Oxford University Press, 1978), 32–45.

4. For a more detailed look at how New Zealand and Australian perceptions of the Pacific differ even from each other see K. R. Howe, "New Zealand's twentieth-century Pacifics: Memories and reflections," *New Zealand Journal of History* 34:1 (2000).

5. For example, Paul Carter, *The Road to Botany Bay: An Essay in Spatial History* (London: Faber and Faber, 1987).

6. Epeli Hau'ofa, "Our sea of islands," *The Contemporary Pacific* 6:1 (1994), 147–161; and his "The Ocean in us," *The Contemporary Pacific* 10:2 (1999), 392–410. See also Nonie Sharp, "Reimagining sea

space: From Grotius to Mabo," *Arena* 7 (1996), 111–129. Reflecting Westerners' differing and sometimes conflicting cultural mapping of Oceania, many islanders too contest outlines; see Eric Waddell, Vijay Naidu, and Epeli Hau'ofa, eds., *A New Oceania: Rediscovering Our Sea of Islands* (Suva: University of the South Pacific, 1994).

7. Howe, "Intellectual discovery."

8. George Boas, *Essays on Primitivism and Related Ideas in the Middle Ages* (New York: Octagon Books, 1978).

9. de Labillardière, *Voyage*, v.

10. Edward B. Tylor, "Phenomena of the Higher Civilisation traceable to a rudimental origin among savage tribes," *Anthropological Review* 5 (1867), 304–305.

11. For example, S. M. Lambert, *A Doctor in Paradise* (London: J. M. Dent and Sons, 1941).

12. Norma McArthur, *Introducing Population Statistics* (Melbourne: Melbourne University Press, 1961).

13. Philip Houghton, *People of the Great Ocean: Aspects of Human Biology of the Early Pacific* (Cambridge: Cambridge University Press, 1996); John Miles, *Infectious Diseases: Colonising the Pacific?* (Dunedin: University of Otago Press, 1997).

14. Still the best foundational survey of island populations is Norma McArthur, *Island Populations of the Pacific* (Canberra: Australian National University Press, 1967).

15. David E. Stannard, *Before the Horror: The Population of Hawai'i on the Eve of Western Contact* (Honolulu: Social Sciences Research Institute, 1989). See also A. W. Crosby, "Hawaiian depopulation as a model for the Amerindian experience," in *Epidemics and Ideas: Essays on the Historical Perception of Pestilence,* ed. Terence Ranger and Paul Slack (Cambridge: Cambridge University Press, 1992), 175–201. A useful critique of Stannard is Andrew F. Bushnell, " 'The Horror' reconsidered: An evaluation of the historical evidence for population decline in Hawaii, 1778–1803," *Pacific Studies* 16:3 (1993), 115–161.

It is worth noting that the preoccupation with the size of contact populations in current issues of redemption/compensation for past colonial injustice and indigenous sovereignty politics are not universal. For example, in Australia more attention is given to the dating of the first human settlement of Australia, and in New Zealand it is neither size of population nor initial settlement dates that form the basis for contestation, but the 1840 Treaty of Waitangi.

16. For useful discussions of these matters for the Pacific and elsewhere see Raeburn Lange, "European medicine in the Cook Islands," in *Disease, Medicine, and Empire,* ed. Roy Macleod and Milton Lewis (Lon-

don: Routledge, 1988), 61–79; Donald Denoon, "Pacific island depopulation: Natural or un-natural," in *New Countries and Old Medicine*, ed. Lynda Bryder and Derek A. Dow (Auckland: Pyramid Press, 1994), 324–339; Stephen J. Kunitz, *Diseases and Social Diversity: The European Impact on the Health of Non-Europeans* (New York: Oxford University Press, 1994), esp. chap. 3; David Arnold, "Medicine and Colonialism," in *Companion Encyclopedia of the History of Medicine*, ed. W. F. Bynum and Roy Porter (London: Routledge, 1993), 1:1393–1416.

17. J. C. Furnas, *Anatomy of Paradise: Hawaii and the Islands of the South Seas* (London: Gollancz, 1948), 385, and passim.

18. J. W. Davidson, *The Study of Pacific History: An Inaugural Lecture Delivered at Canberra on 25 November 1954* (Canberra: Australian National University, 1955).

19. The historiographic literature on Pacific studies is now immense. An excellent bibliography is Clive Moore and Doug Munro, "The nature of Pacific history: A bibliography," in *Reflections on Pacific Historiography*, ed. Doug Munro, a special issue of *The Journal of Pacific Studies* 20 (1996), 155–160. It lists some seventy-five items, most published within the last fifteen years. See also Jocelyn Linnekin, "Contending approaches," in *The Cambridge History of the Pacific Islanders,* ed. Donald Denoon (Cambridge: Cambridge University Press, 1997), 3–36.

20. For example, K. R. Howe, *Where the Waves Fall: A New South Sea Islands History from First Settlement to Colonial Rule* (Sydney: Allen and Unwin, 1984); Deryck Scarr, *The History of the Pacific Islands: Kingdoms of the Reefs* (Melbourne: Macmillan, 1990); I. C. Campbell, *A History of the Pacific Islands* (Christchurch: University of Canterbury Press, 1989).

21. For example, K. R. Howe, Robert C. Kiste, and Brij V. Lal, eds., *Tides of History: The Pacific Islands in the Twentieth Century* (Sydney: Allen and Unwin, 1994); Denoon, ed., *The Cambridge History.*

22. For example, Nicholas Thomas, *Colonialism's Culture: Anthropology, Travel and Government* (Cambridge: Polity Press, 1994). Attention also needs to be drawn again to the significant amount of postcolonial discourse analysis particularly of literary texts relating to the Pacific. See, for example, Edmond, *Representing the South Pacific,* and Vanessa Smith, *Literary Culture.* To some extent such scholars are considering the same or similar issues of postcoloniality as I am, yet in rather different ways, and they come to some rather different conclusions. I have avoided a direct engagement with such work since I am coming from a different perspective and I am concerned specifically with Pacific history and historians. And I sometimes have questions about some of the literary and other nonhistorian scholars' understandings of the Pacific historical and

historiographic contexts in which their own targets are ostensibly based. For example, I am not convinced by Nicholas Thomas' claim, and Edmond's acceptance of it, that there has existed a simplistic dichotomy between a "mindlessly particular conventional colonial history" and a totalizing "colonial discourse theory" (Thomas, 60; Edmond, 11). I do not deny such practices exist. But that is not my understanding of how Pacific history, old or new, has necessarily been written.

23. Henri Baudet, *Paradise on Earth: Some Thoughts on European Images of Non-European Man* (New Haven, Conn.: Yale University Press, 1965).

24. For some discussions of identity see Roger M. Keesing and Robert Tonkinson, eds., *Reinventing Traditional Culture: The Politics of Kastom in Island Melanesia,* special issue of *Mankind* 13 (1982); Margaret Jolly and Nicholas Thomas, eds., *The Politics of Tradition in the Pacific,* special issue of *Oceania* 62 (1993); Geoffrey White and Lamont Lindstrom, eds., *Custom Today,* special issue of *Anthropological Forum* 6 (1993); Vilsoni Hereniko, "Representations of cultural identities," in Howe, Kiste, Lal, eds., *Tides of History,* 406–434; Linnekin, "The ideological world remade," in Denoon, ed., *The Cambridge History,* 397–438.

25. Roger M. Keesing, "Creating the past: Custom and identity in the contemporary Pacific," *The Contemporary Pacific* 1:1 and 2 (1989), 19–42. See also "Dialogue" with Keesing, Haunani-Kay Trask, and Jocelyn Linnekin, ibid., 3:1 (1991), 146–177.

26. Stephanie Lawson, *Tradition versus Democracy in the South Pacific: Fiji, Tonga, and Western Samoa* (Cambridge: Cambridge University Press, 1996), 172.

27. David A. Chappell, "Active agents versus passive victims: Decolonized historiography or problematic paradigm?" *The Contemporary Pacific* 7:2 (1995), 303–326.

28. Merchant, *The Death of Nature.*

29. Atu Emberson-Bain, ed., *Sustainable Development or Malignant Growth? Perspectives of Pacific Island Women* (Suva: Marama Publications, 1994).

30. William C. Clarke, "Learning from the past: Traditional knowledge and sustainable development," *The Contemporary Pacific* 2:2 (1990), 233–253.

31. Clive Ponting, *A Green History of the World* (London: Penguin Books, 1992).

32. David Mackay, "The burden of *Terra Australis:* Experiences of real and imagined lands," in *From Maps to Metaphors,* ed. Robin Fisher and Hugh Johnston (Vancouver: UBC Press, 1993), 263–289.

33. Grove, *Ecology, Climate and Empire,* 3.

34. For example, Anne McClintock, *Imperial Leather: Race, Gender and Sexuality in the Colonial Contest* (New York: Routledge, 1995); Anne McClintock, Aamir Mufti, and Ella Shohat, eds., *Dangerous Liaisons: Gender, Nation, and Postcolonial Perspectives* (Minneapolis: University of Minnesota Press, 1997).

35. Caroline Ralston, "The study of women in the Pacific," *The Contemporary Pacific* 4:1 (1992), 162–175.

36. For example, Alan Bewell, "Constructed places, constructed peoples: Charting the improvement of the female body in the Pacific," in *The South Pacific in the Eighteenth Century,* ed. Jonathan Lamb, 37–54.

37. Harriet Guest, "Looking at women: Forster's observations in the South Pacific," in Forster, *Observations,* ed. Nicholas Thomas, xli–liv.

38. Claudia Knapman, *White Women in Fiji, 1835–1930: The Ruin of Empire?* (Sydney: Allen and Unwin, 1986); Amirah Inglis, *Not a White Woman Safe: Sexual Anxiety and Politics in Port Moresby, 1920–34* (Canberra: Australian National University Press, 1974).

39. Teresia K. Teaiwa, "bikinis and other s/pacific n/oceans," *The Contemporary Pacific* 6:1 (1994), 87–109.

40. For example, Caroline Ralston, "Maori women and the politics of tradition," *The Contemporary Pacific* 5:1 (1993), 23–44; Margaret Jolly, *Women of the Place: Kastom, Colonialism and Gender in Vanuatu* (Camberwell: Harwood Academic Publishers, 1994); Margaret Jolly and Martha Macintyre, eds., *Family and Gender in the Pacific: Domestic Contradictions and the Colonial Impact* (Cambridge: Cambridge University Press, 1989); Jocelyn Linnekin, *Sacred Queens and Women of Consequence: Rank, Gender and Colonialism in the Hawaiian Islands* (Ann Arbor: University of Michigan Press, 1990).

41. C. S. Belshaw, *Changing Melanesia: Social Economics of Culture Contact* (Melbourne: Oxford University Press, 1954); Margaret Mead, *New Lives for Old: Cultural Transformation—Manus, 1928–1953* (New York: Morrow, 1956); H. I. Hogbin, *Experiments in Civilization: The Effects of European Culture on a Native Community of the Solomon Islands* (London: Routledge and K. Paul, 1939).

42. For example, Ranajit Guha, ed., *Subaltern Studies: Writings on South Asian History and Society,* vols. 1–4 (Delhi: Oxford University Press, 1982–1989).

43. For example, Marshall Sahlins, *Islands of History* (Chicago: University of Chicago Press, 1985).

44. Marshall Sahlins, *Historical Metaphors and Mythical Realities: Structure in the Early History of the Sandwich Islands Kingdom* (Ann Arbor: University of Michigan Press, 1981); Sahlins, "Captain James Cook; or, the Dying God," in Sahlins, *Islands of History.*

45. Gananath Obeyesekere, *The Apotheosis of Captain Cook: European Mythmaking in the Pacific* (Princeton, N.J.: Princeton University Press, 1992), 3.

46. Ibid., 177.

47. Sahlins' reply to Obeyesekere is *How "Natives" Think: About Captain Cook, for Example* (Chicago: University of Chicago Press, 1995).

48. Obeyesekere, *Apotheosis*, 21.

49. K. R. Howe, "The making of Cook's death," *Journal of Pacific History* 31:1 (1996), 108–118.

50. For example, David Routledge, "Pacific history as seen from the Pacific islands," *Pacific Studies* 8:2 (1985), 81–99; Chappell, "Active agent."

51. Nicholas Thomas, "Partial texts: Representation, colonialism and agency in Pacific history," *Journal of Pacific History* 15:2 (1990), 139–158; Doug Munro, "Who 'owns' Pacific history?" *Journal of Pacific History* 29:2 (1994), 232–237.

52. H. E. Maude, "Pacific history—past, present and future," *Journal of Pacific History* 6 (1971), 24.

Bibliography

Altmeyer, G. "Three ideas of nature in Canada, 1899–1914." *Journal of Canadian Studies* 11:3 (1976), 21–36.

Amherst, Lord, and Basil Thomson, eds. *The Discovery of the Solomon Islands by Alvaro de Mendana in 1568*. London: Hakluyt Society, 1901.

Arnold, David. "Medicine and colonialism." In *Companion Encyclopedia of the History of Medicine*, ed. W. F. Bynum and Roy Porter, 1: 1393–1416. London: Routledge, 1993.

Asterisk [Robert James Fletcher]. *Isles of Illusion: Letters from the South Seas*. London: Century Hutchinson, 1986.

Bann, Stephen. "From Captain Cook to Neil Armstrong: Colonial exploration and the structure of landscape." In *Reading Landscape: Country, City, Capital*, ed. Simon Pugh, 214–230. Manchester: Manchester University Press, 1990.

Barth, Gunther. *Fleeting Moments: Nature and Culture in American History*. Oxford: Oxford University Press, 1990.

Baudet, Henri. *Paradise on Earth: Some Thoughts on European Images of Non-European Man*. New Haven, Conn.: Yale University Press, 1965.

Beaglehole, J. C., ed. *The "Endeavour" Journal of Joseph Banks 1768–1771*. Vol. 1. Sydney: Angus and Robertson, 1963.

———. *The Voyage of the "Endeavour" 1768–1771*. London: Hakluyt Society, Kraus Reprint, 1988.

Becke, Louis. *By Reef and Palm*. Sydney: Angus and Robertson, 1955.

Belshaw, C. S. *Changing Melanesia: Social Economics of Culture Contact*. Melbourne: Oxford University Press, 1954.

Bendysche, Thomas. *The Anthropological Treatises of Johann Friedrich Blumenbach*. Boston: Milford House, 1973.

Bewell, Alan. "Constructed places, constructed peoples: Charting the improvement of the female body in the Pacific." In *The South Pacific in the Eighteenth Century: Narratives and Myths*, ed. Jonathan Lamb. Special edition of *Eighteenth Century Life* 18:3 (1994), 37–54.

Bloch, Ernst. *The Principle of Hope*. Trans. Neville Plaice et al. 3 vols. Cambridge, Mass.: MIT Press, 1986.

Boas, George. *Essays on Primitivism and Related Ideas in the Middle Ages*. New York: Octagon Books, 1978.

Booth, Douglas. "Healthy, economic, disciplined bodies: Surfbathing and surf lifesaving in Australia and New Zealand, 1890–1950. *New Zealand Journal of History* 32:1 (1998), 43–58.

Botting, Douglas. *Humboldt and the Cosmos*. London: Michael Joseph, 1973.

Bougainville, Louis-Antoine de. *A Voyage Round the World . . . in the Frigate "La Boudeuse" and the Store Ship "L'Etoile."*. . . Trans. J. R. Forster. London: J. Nourse and T. Davies, 1772.

Bowler, Peter J. *Darwinism*. New York: Twayne, 1993.

Brawley, Sean, and Chris Dixon. "'The Hollywood Native': Hollywood's construction of the South Seas and wartime encounters with the South Pacific." *Sites* 27 (1993), 15–29.

Brown, John Macmillan. *Peoples and Problems of the Pacific*. 2 vols. London: T. Fisher Unwin, 1927.

———. *The Riddle of the Pacific*. London: T. Fisher Unwin, 1924.

Buck, Elizabeth. *Paradise Remade: The Politics of Culture and History in Hawai'i*. Philadelphia: Temple University Press, 1993.

Buckle, Henry Thomas. *Introduction to the History of Civilization in England*. London: George Routledge and Sons, 1904.

Burton, John Wear. *The Fiji of Today*. London: Charles H. Kelly, 1910.

Bushnell, Andrew F. "'The Horror' reconsidered: An evaluation of the historical evidence for population decline in Hawaii, 1778–1803." *Pacific Studies* 16:3 (1993), 115–161.

Campbell, I. C. *A History of the Pacific Islands*. Christchurch: University of Canterbury Press, 1989.

Carter, Paul. *The Road to Botany Bay: An Essay in Spatial History*. London: Faber and Faber, 1987.

Chappell, David A. "Active agents versus passive victims: Decolonized historiography or problematic paradigm?" *The Contemporary Pacific: A Journal of Island Affairs* 7:2 (1995), 303–326.

Churchward, James. *The Lost Continent of Mu*. Albuquerque, N.M.: BE Books, [1931], 1991.

Clarke, William C. "Learning from the past: Traditional knowledge and sustainable development." *The Contemporary Pacific: A Journal of Island Affairs* 2:2 (1990), 233–253.

Cilento, R. W. "The depopulation of the Pacific." *Proceedings of the Pan-Pacific Science Congress* 2 (1923), 1395–1399.

Clifford, James, and George E. Marcus, eds. *Writing Culture: The Poetics and Politics of Ethnography.* Berkeley: University of California Press, 1986.

Cohen, J. M. *The Four Voyages of Christopher Columbus.* London: Cresset, 1969.

The Commercial Directory and Tourists' Guide to the South Pacific Islands 1903–4. Sydney: T. B. Dineen, 1904.

Cooper, H. Stonehewer. *Coral Lands.* London: R. Bentley, 1882.

Corbin, Alain. *The Lure of the Sea: The Discovery of the Seaside in the Western World 1750–1840.* Berkeley: University of California Press, 1994.

Crosby, A. W. *Ecological Imperialism: The Biological Expansion of Europe 900–1900.* Cambridge: Cambridge University Press, 1986.

———. "Hawaiian depopulation as a model for the Amerindian experience." In *Epidemics and Ideas: Essays on the Historical Perception of Pestilence,* ed. Terence Ranger and Paul Slack, 175–201. Cambridge: Cambridge University Press, 1992.

Curtin, Philip D. *Death by Migration: Europe's Encounter with the Tropical World in the Nineteenth Century.* Cambridge: Cambridge University Press, 1989.

———. "'The White Man's grave': Image and reality, 1750–1850." *Journal of British Studies* 1:1 (1961), 94–110.

Davidson, J. W. *The Study of Pacific History: An Inaugural Lecture Delivered at Canberra on 25 November 1954.* Canberra: Australian National University, 1955.

Davis, William Morris. "An inductive study of the content of Geography." *Bulletin American Geographical Society* 38 (1906). Reprinted in *Geographical Essays by William Morris Davis,* ed. Douglas Wilson Johnson, 3–22. New York: Dover, 1954.

Daws, Gavan. *A Dream of Islands: Voyages of Self-discovery in the South Seas.* Milton, Queensland: Jacaranda Press, 1980.

Day, A. Grove. *Louis Becke.* New York: Twayne Publishers, 1966.

Day, A. Grove, ed. *Louis Becke: South Sea Supercargo.* Brisbane: Jacaranda Press, n.d.

Defoe, Daniel. *Robinson Crusoe.* London: Everyman's Library, 1964.

Dening, Greg. "History *in* the Pacific." *The Contemporary Pacific: A Journal of Island Affairs* 1:1 and 2 (1989), 134–139.

Denoon, Donald. "Pacific island depopulation: Natural or un-natural?" In *New Countries and Old Medicine,* ed. Lynda Bryder and Derek A. Dow, 324–339. Auckland: Pyramid Press, 1994.

Denoon, Donald, ed. *The Cambridge History of the Pacific Islanders.* Cambridge: Cambridge University Press, 1997.

Dettelbach, Michael. "Global physics and aesthetic empire: Humbolt's physical portrait of the tropics." In *Visions of Empire: Voyages, Botany, and Representations of Nature,* ed. David Philip Miller and Peter Hanns Reill, 258–292. Cambridge: Cambridge University Press, 1996.

Diamond, Jarad. *Guns, Germs and Steel: A Short History of Everybody for the Last 13,000 Years.* London: Vintage, 1998.

———. *The Rise and Fall of the Third Chimpanzee.* London: Radius, 1991.

Douglas, Ngaire. *They Came for Savages: 100 Years of Tourism in Melanesia.* Lismore, NSW: Southern Cross University Press, 1996.

Douglas, Norman, and Ngaire Douglas. "Tourism in the Pacific: Historical factors." In *Tourism in the Pacific: Issues and Cases,* ed. Michael C. Hall and Stephen J. Page, 19–35. London: International Thomson Business Press, 1996.

Duncan, James, and David Ley, eds. *Place/Culture/Representation.* London: Routledge, 1993.

Edmond, Rod. *Representing the South Pacific: Colonial Discourse from Cook to Gauguin.* Cambridge: Cambridge University Press, 1997.

Eisler, William. *The Furthest Shore: Images of Terra Australis from the Middle Ages to Captain Cook.* Cambridge: Cambridge University Press, 1995.

Emberson-Bain, Atu, ed. *Sustainable Development or Malignant Growth? Perspectives of Pacific Island Women.* Suva: Marama Publications, 1994.

Fausett, David. *Images of the Antipodes in the Eighteenth Century: A Study in Stereotyping.* Amsterdam: Rodopi, 1995.

———. *Writing the New World: Imaginary Voyages and Utopias of the Great Southern Land.* Syracuse, N.Y.: Syracuse University Press, 1993.

Fenton, F. D. *Suggestions for a History of the Origins and Migrations of the Maori People.* Auckland: H. Brett, 1885.

Flint, Valerie I. J. *The Imaginative Landscape of Christopher Columbus.* Princeton, N.J.: Princeton University Press, 1992.

Forbes, A. L. A. "On the extinction of certain races of men." *New South Wales Medical Gazette* 3 (1873), 217–321.

Formisano, Luciano, ed. *Letters from a New World: Amerigo Vespucci's Discovery of America.* New York: Marsilio, 1992.

Forster, George. *A Voyage Round the World.* London: B. White, 1777.

Forster, Johann Reinhold. *Observations Made during a Voyage Round the World* [1778], ed. Nicholas Thomas, Harriet Guest, and Michael Dettelbach. Honolulu: University of Hawai'i Press, 1996.

Freeman, Derek. *Margaret Mead and Samoa: The Making and Unmaking of an Anthropological Myth.* Canberra: Australian National University Press, 1983.

Furnas, J. C. *Anatomy of Paradise: Hawaii and the Islands of the South Seas.* London: Gollancz, 1948.

Glacken, Clarence J. *Traces on the Rhodian Shore: Nature and Culture in Western Thought from Ancient Times to the End of the Eighteenth Century.* Berkeley: University of California Press, 1967.

Goldie, Terry. *Fear and Temptation: The Image of the Indigene in Canadian, Australian, and New Zealand Literature.* Montreal: McGill-Queen's University Press, 1993.

Goleman, Daniel. *Emotional Intelligence.* London: Bloomsbury, 1996.

Greenblatt, Stephen. *Marvelous Possessions: The Wonder of the New World.* Chicago: University of Chicago Press, 1991.

Grove, Richard H. *Ecology, Climate and Empire.* Cambridge: White Horse Press, 1997.

————. *Green Imperialism: Colonial Expansion, Tropical Island Edens and the Origins of Environmentalism 1600–1860.* Cambridge: Cambridge University Press, 1995.

Guest, Harriet. "Looking at women: Forster's observations in the South Pacific." In J. R. Forster, *Observations made During a Voyage Round the World,* ed. Nicholas Thomas, Harriet Guest, and Michael Dettelbach, xli–liv. Honolulu: University of Hawai'i Press, 1996.

Haddon, Alfred C. *History of Anthropology.* New York: G. P. Putnam's Sons, 1910.

Haeckel, Ernst. *The History of Creation, Or the Development of the Earth and Its Inhabitants by the Action of Natural Causes.* London: Kegan Paul, Trench, 1883.

Epeli Hau'ofa. "The Ocean in us." *The Contemporary Pacific: A Journal of Island Affairs* 10:2 (1999), 392–410.

————. "Our sea of islands." *The Contemporary Pacific: A Journal of Island Affairs* 6:1 (1994), 147–161.

Healy, Chris. *From the Ruins of Colonialism: History as Social Memory.* Melbourne: Cambridge University Press, 1997.

Hereniko, Vilsoni. "Representations of cultural identities." In *Tides of History: The Pacific Islands in the Twentieth Century,* ed. K. R. Howe, Robert C. Kiste, and Brij V. Lal, 406–434. Sydney: Allen and Unwin, 1994.

Heyerdahl, Thor. *Fatu Hiva: Back to Nature.* London: George Allen and Unwin, 1974.

Hirsch, Eric, and Michael O'Hanlon, eds. *The Anthropology of Landscape: Perspectives on Place and Space.* Oxford: Clarendon Press, 1995.

Hoare, Michael. *The Tactless Philosopher: Johann Reinhold Forster 1729–1798.* Melbourne: Hawthorn Press, 1976.

Hogbin, H. I. *Experiments in Civilization: The Effects of European Culture on a Native Community of the Solomon Islands.* London: Routledge and K. Paul, 1939.

Houghton, Philip. *People of the Great Ocean: Aspects of Human Biology of the Early Pacific.* Cambridge: Cambridge University Press, 1996.

Howe, K. R. "The fate of the 'savage' in Pacific historiography." *New Zealand Journal of History* 11:2 (1977), 137–154.

———. "The intellectual discovery and exploration of Polynesia." In *From Maps to Metaphors: The Pacific World of George Vancouver,* ed. Robin Fisher and Hugh Johnston, 245–262. Vancouver: UBC Press, 1993.

———. "The making of Cook's death." *Journal of Pacific History* 31:1 (1996), 108–118.

———. "New Zealand's twentieth-century Pacifics: Memories and reflections." *New Zealand Journal of History* 34:1 (2000).

———. "Some origins and migrations of ideas leading to the Aryan Polynesian theories of Abraham Fornander and Edward Tregear." *Pacific Studies* 11:2 (1988), 67–81.

———. *Where the Waves Fall: A New South Sea Islands History from First Settlement to Colonial Rule.* Sydney: Allen and Unwin, 1984.

Howe, K. R., Robert C. Kiste, and Brij V. Lal, eds. *Tides of History: The Pacific Islands in the Twentieth Century.* Sydney: Allen and Unwin, 1994.

Humboldt, Alexander von. *Cosmos: A Sketch of the Physical Description of the Universe.* Vol. 1. Trans. E. C. Otté. London: Henry G. Bohn, 1864.

Huntington, Ellsworth. "Climate and the evolution of civilization." In *The Evolution of Earth and Man,* ed. George Alfred Baitsell, 330–383. New Haven, Conn.: Yale University Press, 1929.

Inglis, Amirah. *Not a White Woman Safe: Sexual Anxiety and Politics in Port Moresby, 1920–34.* Canberra: Australian National University Press, 1974.

Jack-Hinton, Colin. *The Search for the Islands of Solomon 1567–1838.* Oxford: Clarendon Press, 1969.

Jane, Cecil, trans. *The Journal of Christopher Columbus.* London: Orion Press, 1960.

Jardine, N., J. A. Secord, and E. C. Spary, eds. *Cultures of Natural History.* Cambridge: Cambridge University Press, 1996.

Johnson, Martin. *Through the South Seas with Jack London.* Cedar Springs, Mich.: Wolf House Books, 1972.

Johnston, R. J. *Geography and Geographers: Anglo-American Human Geography since 1945.* 2d ed. Baltimore: Edward Arnold, 1985.

Jolly, Margaret. *Women of the Place: Kastom, Colonialism and Gender in Vanuatu.* Camberwell: Harwood Academic Publishers, 1994.

Jolly, Margaret, and Martha Macintyre, eds. *Family and Gender in the Pacific: Domestic Contradictions and the Colonial Impact.* Cambridge: Cambridge University Press, 1989.

Jolly, Margaret, and Nicholas Thomas, eds. *The Politics of Tradition in the Pacific.* Special issue of *Oceania* 62 (1993).

Keesing, Roger M. "Creating the past: Custom and identity in the contemporary Pacific." *The Contemporary Pacific: A Journal of Island Affairs* 1:1 and 2 (1989), 19–42.

Keesing, Roger M., Haunani-Kay Trask, and Jocelyn Linnekin. "Dialogue." *The Contemporary Pacific: A Journal of Island Affairs* 3:1 (1991), 146–177.

Keesing, Roger M., and Robert Tonkinson, eds. *Reinventing Traditional Culture: The Politics of Kastom in Island Melanesia.* Special issue of *Mankind* 13 (1982).

Kellner, L. *Alexander von Humboldt.* London: Oxford University Press, 1963.

Kidd, Benjamin. *The Control of the Tropics.* London: Macmillan, 1898.

Knapman, Claudia. *White Women in Fiji, 1835–1930: The Ruin of Empire?* Sydney: Allen and Unwin, 1986.

Kuklick, Henrika. "The color blue: From research in the Torres Strait to an ecology of human behaviour." In *Evolutionary Theory and the Natural History of the Pacific: Darwin's Laboratory,* ed. Roy MacLeod and Philip E. Rehbock, 339–367. Honolulu: University of Hawai'i Press, 1994.

Kunitz, Stephen J. *Diseases and Social Diversity: The European Impact on the Health of Non-Europeans,* esp. chap. 3. New York: Oxford University Press, 1994.

Labillardière, J. J. H de. *Voyage in Search of La Pérouse, Performed by the Order of the Constituent Assembly during the Years 1791, 1792, 1793, and 1794.* London: Stockdale, 1800.

A Lady Member of the Melanesian Mission. *The Isles That Wait.* London: Society for Promoting Christian Knowledge, 1915.

Lamb, Jonathan, ed. *The South Pacific in the Eighteenth Century: Narratives and Myths.* Special edition of *Eighteenth Century Life* 18:3 (1994).

Lambert, S. M. *A Doctor in Paradise.* London: J. M. Dent and Sons, 1941.

Lange, Raeburn. "European medicine in the Cook Islands." In *Disease, Medicine, and Empire,* ed. Roy Macleod and Milton Lewis, 61–79. London: Routledge, 1988.

Laracy, Eugenie, and Hugh Laracy. "Beatrice Grimshaw: Pride and prejudice in Papua." *Journal of Pacific History* 12:3–4 (1977), 154–175.

Lawson, Stephanie. *Tradition versus Democracy in the South Pacific: Fiji,
Tonga, and Western Samoa.* Cambridge: Cambridge University Press,
1996.

Leslie, John. *The End of the World: The Science and Ethics of Human
Extinction.* London: Routledge, 1996.

Linnekin, Jocelyn. "Contending approaches" and "The ideological world
remade." In *The Cambridge History of the Pacific Islanders,* ed. Donald Denoon, 3–36; 397–438. Cambridge: Cambridge University Press,
1997.

———. *Sacred Queens and Women of Consequence: Rank, Gender and
Colonialism in the Hawaiian Islands.* Ann Arbor: University of Michigan Press, 1990.

Livingstone, David N. "Climate's moral economy: Science, race and place
in post-Darwinian British and American geography." In *Geography
and Empire,* ed. Anne Godlewska and Neil Smith, 132–154. Oxford:
Blackwell, 1994.

Lopez, Barry. *Arctic Dreams: Imagination and Desire in a Northern Landscape.* New York: Charles Scribner, 1986.

Loxley, Diana. *Problematic Shores: The Literature of Islands.* New York:
St. Martin's Press, 1990.

McArthur, Norma. *Introducing Population Statistics.* Melbourne: Melbourne University Press, 1961.

———. *Island Populations of the Pacific.* Canberra: Australian National
University Press, 1967.

McClintock, Anne. *Imperial Leather: Race, Gender and Sexuality in the
Colonial Contest.* New York: Routledge, 1995.

McClintock, Anne, Aamir Mufti, and Ella Shohat, eds. *Dangerous Liaisons: Gender, Nation, and Postcolonial Perspectives.* Minneapolis:
University of Minnesota Press, 1997.

McGuire, Paul. *Westward the Course: The New World of Oceania.* Melbourne: Oxford University Press, 1942.

Mackay, David. "The burden of *Terra Australis:* Experiences of real and
imagined lands." In *From Maps to Metaphors: The Pacific World of
George Vancouver,* ed. Robin Fisher and Hugh Johnston, 263–289.
Vancouver: UBC Press, 1993.

McKibben, Bill. *The End of Nature.* London: Viking, 1990.

MacLeod, Roy, and Philip E. Rehbock, eds. *Evolutionary Theory and the
Natural History of the Pacific: Darwin's Laboratory.* Honolulu: University of Hawai'i Press, 1994.

———. *Nature in Its Greatest Extent: Western Science in the Pacific.*
Honolulu: University of Hawai'i Press, 1988.

Maitland, Gordon. "The two sides of the camera lens: Nineteenth century photography and the indigenous people of the South Pacific." *Photofile South Pacific,* 1988, 47–60.

Malinowski, Bronislaw. *Argonauts of the Western Pacific: An Account of Native Enterprise and Adventure in the Archipelagoes of Melanesian New Guinea.* London: George Routledge, 1932.

———. *A Diary in the Strict Sense of the Term.* London: Routledge and Kegan Paul, 1967.

Markham, Clements, ed. *The Voyages of Pedro Fernandez de Quiros 1595 to 1604.* London: Hakluyt Society, 1904.

Maude, H. E. "Pacific history—past, present and future." *Journal of Pacific History* 6 (1971), 3–24.

Mead, Margaret. *Coming of Age in Samoa: A Study of Adolescence and Sex in Primitive Societies.* Harmondsworth: Penguin, 1963.

———. *New Lives for Old: Cultural Transformation—Manus, 1928–1953.* New York: Morrow, 1956.

Meek, Ronald L. *Social Science and the Ignoble Savage.* Cambridge: Cambridge University Press, 1976.

Merchant, Carolyn. *The Death of Nature: Women, Ecology, and the Scientific Revolution.* New York: Harper, 1990.

Miles, John. *Infectious Diseases: Colonising the Pacific?* Dunedin: University of Otago Press, 1997.

Miller, David Philip, and Peter Hanns Reill, eds. *Visions of Empire: Voyages, Botany, and Representations of Nature.* Cambridge: Cambridge University Press, 1996.

Mithen, Steve. *The Prehistory of the Mind: A Search for the Origins of Art, Religion and Science.* London: Thames and Hudson, 1996.

Montesquieu, Baron de. *The Spirit of Laws* [1748]. Trans. Thomas Nugent. New York: Hafner, 1949.

Moore, Clive, and Doug Munro. "The nature of Pacific history: A bibliography." In *Reflections on Pacific Historiography,* ed. Doug Munro, 155–160. Special issue of *The Journal of Pacific Studies* 20 (1996).

Munro, Doug. "Who 'owns' Pacific history?" *Journal of Pacific History* 29:2 (1994), 232–237.

Nabhan, Gary Paul. *The Geography of Childhood: Why Children Need Wild Places.* Boston: Beacon Press, 1994.

Nash, Dennison. *Anthropology of Tourism.* Oxford: Pergamon, 1996.

Nash, Roderick. *Wilderness and the American Mind.* Rev. ed. New Haven, Conn.: Yale University Press, 1973.

Neil, Tom. *An Island to Oneself: The Story of Six Years on a Desert Island.* London: Collins, 1966.

Neubauer, Peter B., and Alexander Neubauer. *Nature's Thumbprint: The New Genetics of Personality.* New York: Addison-Wesley, 1990.

Nye, Robert A. "Degeneration and the medical model of culture crisis in the French *Belle Epoque.*" In *Political Symbolism in Modern Europe,* ed. Seymour Drescher et al., 19–41. New Brunswick: Transaction Books, 1982.

Obeyesekere, Gananath. *The Apotheosis of Captain Cook: European Mythmaking in the Pacific.* Princeton, N.J.: Princeton University Press, 1992.

O'Connor, Kaori, ed. *"Pacific Tales" by Louis Becke* [1897]. London: KPI, 1987.

Oelschlaeger, Max. *The Idea of Wilderness: From Prehistory to the Age of Ecology.* New Haven, Conn.: Yale University Press, 1991.

O'Hanlon, Redmond. *Joseph Conrad and Charles Darwin: The Influence of Scientific Thought on Conrad's Fiction.* Edinburgh: Salamander Press, 1984.

Park, Geoff. *Nga Ururoa: The Groves of Life: Ecology and History in a New Zealand Landscape.* Wellington: Victoria University Press, 1995.

Phelan, Nancy. *Pieces of Heaven: In the South Seas.* St. Lucia: University of Queensland Press, 1996.

Pick, Daniel. *Faces of Degeneration: A European Disorder, c.1848–c.1918.* Cambridge: Cambridge University Press, 1993.

Pinker, Steven. *How the Mind Works.* New York: Norton, 1997.

Pitt-Rivers, George Henry Lane-Fox. *The Clash of Culture and the Contact of Races.* London: George Routledge and Sons, 1927.

Plotkin, Henry. *The Nature of Knowledge: Concerning Adaptations, Instinct and the Evolution of Intelligence.* London: Penguin, 1994.

Ponder, Winifred. *An Idler in the Islands.* Sydney: Cornstalk Publishing, 1924.

Ponting, Clive. *A Green History of the World.* London: Penguin Books, 1992.

Prest, John. *The Garden of Eden: The Botanic Garden and the Re-creation of Paradise.* New Haven, Conn.: Yale University Press, 1981.

Price, A. Grenfell. *White Settlers in the Tropics.* New York: American Geographical Society, 1939.

Puxley, W. Lavallin. *Green Islands in Glittering Seas.* London: George Allen and Unwin, 1925.

Quammen, David. *The Song of the Dodo: Island Biogeography in an Age of Extinctions.* New York: Scribner, 1996.

Raban, Jonathan, ed. *The Oxford Book of the Sea.* Oxford: Oxford University Press, 1992.

[Ragotte, Freda, and Ron Crocomb, eds.] *Pacific Tourism as Islanders See It.* Suva: Institute of Pacific Studies, 1980.

Ralston, Caroline. "Maori women and the politics of tradition." *The Contemporary Pacific: A Journal of Island Affairs* 5:1 (1993), 23–44.

————. "The study of women in the Pacific." *The Contemporary Pacific: A Journal of Island Affairs* 4:1 (1992), 162–175.

Rennie, Neil. *Far-fetched Facts: The Literature of Travel and the Idea of the South Seas.* Oxford: Clarendon Press, 1995.

Rivers, W. H. R., ed. *Essays on the Depopulation of Melanesia.* Cambridge: Cambridge University Press , 1922.

Roberts, Stephen H. *Population Problems of the Pacific.* London: George Routledge, 1927.

Ross, Andrew. "Cultural preservation in the Polynesia of the Latter-Day Saints." In Andrew Ross, *The Chicago Gangster Theory of Life: Nature's Debt to Society,* 21–98. London: Verso, 1994.

Routledge, David. "Pacific history as seen from the Pacific islands." *Pacific Studies* 8:2 (1985), 81–99.

Russell, M. *Polynesia: A History of the South Seas.* London: T. Nelson, 1853.

Sahlins, Marshall. *Historical Metaphors and Mythical Realities: Structure in the Early History of the Sandwich Islands Kingdom.* Ann Arbor: University of Michigan Press, 1981.

————. *How "Natives" Think: About Captain Cook, for Example.* Chicago: University of Chicago Press, 1995.

————. *Islands of History.* Chicago: University of Chicago Press, 1985.

St. Johnston, T. R. *The Islands of the Pacific, or the Children of the Sun.* New York: Appleton, 1921.

Scarr, Deryck. *The History of the Pacific Islands: Kingdoms of the Reefs.* Melbourne: Macmillan, 1990.

Schama, Simon. *Landscape and Memory.* London: Harper Collins, 1995.

Schmitt, Peter J. *Back to Nature: The Arcadian Myth in Urban America.* New York: Oxford University Press, 1969.

Sharp, Nonie. "Reimagining sea space: From Grotius to Mabo." *Arena* 7 (1996), 111–129.

Shephard, Alastair. "The Coral Route story: A history of TEAL's flying boat service in the Pacific 1950–1960." M.A. thesis, Auckland University, 1994.

Smith, Bernard. *The European Vision and the South Pacific 1768–1850: A Study in the History of Art and Ideas.* London: Oxford University Press, 1960.

————. *Imagining the Pacific: In the Wake of the Cook Voyages.* New Haven, Conn.: Yale University Press, 1992.

Smith, S. Percy. *Hawaiki: The Original Home of the Maoris.* Christchurch: Whitcombe and Tombs, 1904.

Smith, Valerie L. *Hosts and Guests: The Anthropology of Tourism.* 2d ed. Philadelphia: University of Pennsylvania Press, 1989.

Smith, Vanessa. *Literary Culture and the Pacific: Nineteenth Century Textual Encounters*. Cambridge: Cambridge University Press, 1998.

Spate, O. H. K. "The Pacific as an artefact." In *The Changing Pacific: Essays in Honour of H. E. Maude,* ed. Niel Gunson, 32–45. Melbourne: Oxford University Press, 1978.

———. *Paradise Found and Lost*. Canberra: Australian National University Press, 1988.

———. " 'South Sea' to 'Pacific Ocean': A note on nomenclature." *Journal of Pacific History* 12:4 (1977), 205–211.

———. *The Spanish Lake*. Canberra: Australian National University Press, 1979.

Spufford, Francis. *I May Be Some Time: Ice and the English Imagination*. London: Faber and Faber, 1996.

Stannard, David E. *Before the Horror: The Population of Hawai'i on the Eve of Western Contact*. Honolulu: Social Sciences Research Institute, 1989.

Steven, Anna, ed. *Pirating the Pacific: Images of Travel, Trade and Tourism*. Sydney: Powerhouse Publishing, 1993.

Stevenson, Robert Louis. *In the South Seas* [1896]. London: Hogarth Press, 1987.

Stocking, George W. *Victorian Anthropology*. New York: Free Press, 1987.

———. *After Tylor: British Social Anthropology 1888–1951*. Madison: University of Wisconsin Press, 1995.

Tatham, George. "Geography in the nineteenth century" and "Environmentalism and possibilism." In *Geography in the Twentieth Century: A Study of Growth, Fields, Techniques, Aims and Trends,* ed. Griffith Taylor, 28–69; 128–162. London: Methuen, 1960.

Taylor, Griffith. "Racial geography." In *Geography in the Twentieth Century: A Study of Growth, Fields, Techniques, Aims and Trends,* ed. Griffith Taylor, 433–462a. London: Methuen, 1960.

Teaiwa, Teresia K. "bikinis and other s/pacific n/oceans." *The Contemporary Pacific: A Journal of Island Affairs* 6:1 (1994), 87–109.

Theroux, Paul. *The Happy Isles of Oceania: Paddling the Pacific*. London: Hamish Hamilton, 1992.

Thomas, Keith. *Man and the Natural World: Changing Attitudes in England 1500–1800*. London: Allen Lane, 1983.

Thomas, Nicholas. *Colonialism's Culture: Anthropology, Travel and Government*. Cambridge: Polity Press, 1994.

———. "Partial texts: Representation, colonialism and agency in Pacific history." *Journal of Pacific History* 15:2 (1990), 139–158.

Thompson, Christina A. "Anthropology's Conrad: Malinowski in the tropics and what he read." *Journal of Pacific History* 30:1 (1995), 53–75.

Thomson, Basil. *The Fijians: A Study of the Decay of Custom*. London: Dawsons, [1908], 1968.

Tylor, Edward B. "Phenomena of the higher civilisation traceable to a rudimental origin among savage tribes." *Anthropological Review* 5 (1867), 304–305.

———. *Primitive Culture: Researches into the Development of Mythology, Philosophy, Religion, Art, and Custom*. 2 vols. London: John Murray, 1871.

Urry, John. *The Tourist Gaze: Leisure and Travel in Contemporary Societies*. London: Sage, 1990.

Visher, Stephen Sargent. "Climatic influences." In *Geography in the Twentieth Century: A Study of Growth, Fields, Techniques, Aims and Trends,* ed. Griffith Taylor, 196–220. London: Methuen, 1960.

Waddell, Eric, Vijay Naidu, and Epeli Hau'ofa, eds. *A New Oceania: Rediscovering Our Sea of Islands*. Suva: University of the South Pacific, 1994.

White, Geoffrey, and Lamont Lindstrom, eds. *Custom Today*. Special issue of *Anthropological Forum* 6 (1993).

Whitson, T. W., ed. *The Tourists' Vade Mecum (Illustrated), Being a Handbook to the Services of the Union Steamship Company. . . Together with an Index Guide*. Dunedin: Union Steam Ship Company of New Zealand, 1912.

Williams, F. E. "Creed of a government anthropologist." In *"The Vailala Madness" and Other Essays,* ed. Erik Schwimmer, 396–418. St. Lucia: University of Queensland Press, 1976.

Williams, Glyndwr. "Buccaneers, castaways, and satirists: The South Seas in the English consciousness before 1750." *The South Pacific in the Eighteenth Century: Narratives and Myths,* ed. Jonathan Lamb. Special edition of *Eighteenth Century Life* 18:3 (1994), 114–128.

———. *The Great South Sea: English Voyages and Encounters 1570–1750*. New Haven, Conn.: Yale University Press, 1997.

Williams, Raymond. "Ideas of Nature." *Ecology, the Shaping Enquiry,* ed. Jonathan Benthall, 146–164. London: Longman, 1972.

Wilson, Alexander. *The Culture of Nature: North American Landscape from Disney to Exxon Valdez*. Cambridge, Mass.: Blackwell, 1992.

Wright, Olive, ed. *New Zealand 1826–1827 from the French of Dumont D'Urville*. Wellington: O. Wright, 1950.

Index

About the Author

K. R. HOWE is a major and longstanding contributor to Pacific history and historiography. Among his previous books are *Where the Waves Fall: A New South Sea Islands History* (1984), *Singer in a Songless Land: A Life of Edward Tregear* (1991), and (co-editor) *Tides of History: The Pacific Islands in the Twentieth Century* (1994). He has a Personal Chair in History at Massey University's Albany Campus in Auckland, New Zealand.